Prime Mincer

1.2

Summer 2011

Subscriptions: $27 for 1 year (3 issues). Inquire for international and institutional rates.

Submissions are accepted year round.

For more info regarding subscriptions, submissions, general rants, raves or anything else, please visit the website.

www.primemincer.com

ISBN-13: 978-0615493855
ISSN-10: 0615493858

Cover Painting by Annie Strong.

Peter Lucas—Managing Editor
Abigail Wheetley—Fiction Editor, Co-Managing Editor
Amy Graziano—Poetry Editor
Andrew Harnish—Fiction Reader
John Stanford Owen—Poetry Reader
Jessica Easto—Proofreader, Master of Chicago Style, Hater of Double Spaces After Periods.

Also, as always, we would like to thank Dexter Wheetley, Emily Wheetley and Jacob Lucas. You kids rock.

Contents

The Paper House

There once was a paper man who lived in a paper house. He had 68 clocks—or 67—it doesn't matter. Each one had a different face.

Some had roman numerals, others numbers, some were just blank, with two vexing hands, a big one and a little one, perplexing young minds in search of glowing digits and instant gratification.

None of them ticked, or tocked, or told the correct time, except for a single second twice each day.

The paper man never looked at his clocks. He never wound them, and they never spoke to him. He was a quiet man who never wound his life. He waited, instead, as the teeth in the wheels would find their mates and push time forward in a fixed inevitability.

Happiness was a foreign word, like *horloge*, or *urb*. There was no understanding to it, no comprehension, no guess. It didn't matter.

Every day, at noon, he would rise from a 12 to 14 hour nap. It wasn't sleep. He never slept, only closed his eyes and lay perfectly still. He said he hadn't been asleep—ever. And he would eat. Though he said he never ate—ever. He would shuffle to the refrigerator, pull the massive stainless steel door open just enough to study, yet again, the contents. Something, anything, would catch his eye, and he would take it from the safe confines of the rubber coated shelf and place it carefully on the polished granite countertop. There was a methodology involved.

He would shift his eating to whatever temporary commitment he had heard about that day, and about which had become an instant expert. No bread, more fruit, more vegetables, less dairy, more dairy, whole grains, no grains, only food that is blue, orange, green. It made perfect nonsense. He exercised by riding a bicycle 127 feet to the mailbox, and back again—sure to cause flushing and a brief case of heavy breathing. Sometimes he would play his fake drums, which sounded like real drums in his headphones, but sounded like sticks along a picket fence outside of that private world.

If anyone would come to the paper door at the front of the paper house and ring the silent doorbell, the paper man would not answer. He would hide. The lights were dim inside the paper house and a plan was in place on how to best appear not at home. No noise was allowed until the interloper was safely away. No matter what they wanted, it didn't matter.

The paper man never gave to charity, never spoke kind words or offered a helping hand without astute calculation involved. Every move, every thought, every effort had to travel back to him. There had to be a reason, an advantage, a positioning that served an inherent benefit. He worked silence like a naked violin. And he could vanish, standing in the center of an empty room. The art of invisibility took him years to perfect.

Butter-yellow walls were inside the paper house. Innocuous, clean, dangerously friendly—the walls whispered in monotone undistinguishable words that shaved off layers of skin.

One day, the paper man was feeling particularly blank. He ventured from the paper house, driving his car designed specifically as a disguise, and went to see his doctor. The doctor was a pen. Shocked to see how blank the paper man had become, he wrote out many long words, as if paid by the syllable, and covered the paper man with all sorts of things to make him feel.

The paper man, feeling especially special because of all the long words that were now a part of him, went to the woman with the bottles. She handed him 13 brown bottles and four white ones. He unfolded with pride. The bottles would make him feel better about being a paper man living in a paper house with 68 clocks—or 67.

At home in his paper house, he counted out the contents of each bottle with the precision of a clock, and noted the purpose of each tiny pill. One would remind him to breathe, the other would stop him from breathing too much; another would tell him he has a soul, and the next would put it to sleep. Each was vital to his survival inside the paper house.

One day, the paper man met…a woman. She was not made of paper, but instead was made of skin and bone; she carried her heart on her back, for it was heavy, but evenly distributed in two separate pieces. He sat behind the safety of his computer and saw her on the internet. He never had to leave his paper house to find the girl of his dreams. They arranged to meet.

He painted himself blue, disguised himself in his car and drove to an agreed upon location. There, she sat at a tiny round table, nursing a tall cup of an exotic herbal tea, awaiting his arrival. She had long blonde hair that captured the beams of the streetlights and bent them into the natural wave. Her eyes were 17 colors all at once, shifting like ocean waves, depending on her mood. Painted by single-thread brushes dipped in sadness, they whispered stories between blinks. She wore a loose, gray-flannel shirt over jeans, and she sat on one leg, like a teenager, or a woman one-third her age. He immediately noticed how she carried her heart in two separate pieces on her back. Interesting, he thought, as he approached like a snake. She smiled.

He looked into her many-colored eyes and saw they were brown. And he couldn't help but notice her accent as she spoke. He asked where she was from. She told him she grew up in a small town called Optimism. She said the town no longer existed, but she remembered it well enough.

The paper man didn't buy any tea. He wasn't there to drink tea; he was there to meet a woman. The woman, remembering her hometown, tore open two tiny pink packets of hope and sprinkled them in her tea. For some reason she needed it sweeter right then.

When they went to his paper house, she found the construction interesting. It was very heavy on one side, weighted by all that was his. The other side was empty. The paper man was very anxious and wanted to make a good impression. His house suddenly felt very empty to him, and he needed to fill it up.

When the woman entered, the butter-yellow walls rippled with delight. They had never seen a soul before. They chattered just a little louder. They spoke in tongues. The house took a breath. One piece of the woman's two-piece heart ached a little at the emptiness. The house was fluent in seven languages, while the paper man had little to say.

They went to the bedroom. The paper man turned her around and grabbed her breasts. He was alone in the room. The woman needed to be touched, even by paper hands. The paper man crawled onto his bed. The woman removed both pieces of her heart and placed them on the floor. There was no room for them in the bed. She climbed in and turned away from him, and the paper man wrapped all around her. She closed her eyes until he finished. It took nine minutes and fourteen seconds. She counted in her head. Her lips felt neglected.

He rolled from the bed, straightened out his wrinkles, and left the room. The woman slipped off of the sheets, reattached her hearts, and went about her day.

In two months, the paper man turned to the woman and told her he loved her. Nothing had changed. She told him one of her hearts didn't want to hear that and it ached. He said the yellow walls missed her and the emptiness had grown loud. He convinced her to stay at the paper house with him. She felt for the empty house, there was so much missing. She agreed but couldn't talk of love. Her hearts wouldn't have it.

She brought things to the paper house: color, music, air, all filled the rooms. She brought dogs and friends, laughter, food. She filled in empty corners and opened books. She worked at making it into a home. It had never been a home. It was a prostitute of namable value. It sometimes would creek and moan, and whisper paper wishes. She could hear it all. The paper man could not.

Their life together was imperfect. He withdrew into a desk drawer and couldn't be found for days at a time. He loved the internet and television. They served him false truths that tasted good and were filled with empty calories. Now the woman could do all the living the paper man did not want to do. She could move her legs, and wash a dish; she could pet the dogs and wipe the counter. She could prepare food and make it lovely, and he would close his eyes and seek his thoughtless methodology of eating.

It wasn't long before both halves of the woman's heart were aching. She was growing thirsty and hungry. Her lips were angry at her, shrinking in neglect; she could no longer speak. She kept thinking of her hometown, and stayed a little longer. Until one night the house and she started talking. She said how much she hated it there. The house said for her to save herself from a fate like death. She went to the paper man and, as he gazed at the television and the computer at the same time, said she was leaving. But it didn't stop there. The house egged her on. The more she spoke, the more her lips filled with sweet moisture. The house spoke in all seven languages at once.

The paper man just stared at the television and computer. He crinkled a little. The woman begged him to hear her. The paper house begged him to hear it. They joined their sounds, louder and louder, until the paper man could only hear them, and not the television or the computer.

He finally looked at the woman and read a prepared statement. He told her how he never loved her. He told her she was wrong in every way. He called her names she'd heard before. They were mean and stupid names, names that had nothing to do with truth. They were names for other things, other parts of the body, other women, other creatures. The names slammed against her like a bullets. They struck her like lightning. They sliced her like razor blades on open wounds and both pieces of her heart fell from her back and shattered on the floor. They were just too heavy for her anymore.

The house kept talking, but the woman fell silent. The paper man stormed about, folding and unfolding, tearing at his corners, kicking the dogs and the paper house. The woman looked at her shattered hearts on the floor and cried. The dogs cried. The butter-yellow walls cried. And the paper man disappeared, as invisibility was his specialty.

A week later, he returned. He had found a pen and had written he was right. His previous silence was nothing compared to the silence he now spoke. It was thick and dark and smelled badly. It oozed from the walls, staining them. The paper house lost all light and the walls smothered beneath the uneven weight. The woman, now without her hearts, sat silently in a tiny room where she had moved all her colors, music, and air. The dogs forced their way in like panicked citizens vying for a fallout shelter. The friends stopped coming and the laughter ended. The food became bitter.

And the paper man returned to the doctor who was a pen, and had him write more long words like *minocycline* and *amlodipine* to stop him from feeling. Then everything would be fine.

Now, the woman sits in her tiny room, with the dogs and the air and the colors, and the butter-yellow walls have decided to shave off skin again. She has nowhere to go without her hearts. Her friends have all disappeared and forgotten. The stench is unbearable, but sometimes she opens the window and remembers there's a world outside where people live.

Io That First Winter

Winter seemed never ending with its crows,
lumped clouds, and sifting snow, its frantic finches
and its jay who screamed *thief, thief* as the glazed
saplings fell along the buckled asphalt. Beyond
the border, in that far country, the sky stretched
to the color of wet steel, water pooled in the cows'
tracks and footsteps echoed across the slick boards
laid against the mud but still I folded the soft-edged
maps, packed away the guides, the compass,
the square, dismissed the proofs and theorems,
the very idea of a pivot point and drove from the city
and its biting flies which never slept. Closed doors
of houses with their many eyes of glass clasped shut
whizzed past as I clamored from packs of dumped dogs
howling sorrow into the night and cats who leapt
from the storm drains' grates and with one swift
neck-breaking claw, snatched the acorn-busy squirrels,
those bundles of chittery fur for whom living
must seem like nothing more than moments
piled on moments of sheer, terrifying luck.
Which is how I felt—except for the luck—
when I moved into the half-collapsed
greenhouse. That's how it was that winter. Gravel
slivered in ice, plant pallets feathered with mold,
bare-boned limbs of trees leaning over fields strewn
with stubble. I settled in, solitude growing exact.
Peacocks cried, ever-watchful tails fanned
as grasshoppers chewed their way up from their cold
graves and all the roots tunneled underground, iris anxious
to rise above the knives of themselves, hyacinths sloughing
off old skin, readying to burst forth, while Callisto,
that Great Bear, slogged on across heaven's horizon.

Two Hundred Thousand Birds in the Season of Horns and Exhaust

In one month blue-eyed grass will wink from every roadside
and yellow loosestrife sway in ditches,
                                        though now in late winter
clumped clay in the disced fields heaves with freeze and thaw
as I mix buckets of rotted sawdust, bone meal, and loam
and center the delicate seeds in bleach-scoured bedding flats
until it's dark and time to scurry the night's drained streets
for the Greek-owned Italian restaurant where, even before
I screech into the parking lot, a single sub,
                                        veal parmigiani,
bread crisped from the massive gas ovens,
cheese dripping onto the Styrofoam container
the cook slides it into, like a body into a coffin,
waits for me to take it,
                    small offering,
and drive it through the city's maze to beer-and vomit-stinking
fraternity row.

It seems strange to me,
                    surreal,
to pick up a phone and have fully cooked food delivered
to your door in minutes, though Big Mike, cook,
                                        second-generation Greek,
tells me this is *progress*.

Gas hovers at a dollar per as I fill my tank,
readying for the late night rush, bars closed,
drunk students stumbling home,
ordering pizzas
                we hope to get to them before they pass out.

The radio interrupts its own blast of hard rock
to the hungry cars at the gas pumps,
an oil spill, the captain's name,
                              Hazelwood,
beautiful, like a forest full of sun-torched trees,
like the two thousand acres
the greenhouse juts up against,

though now in late winter bare branches scratch
against the sky and blackberry brambles
encased in ice tangle in barbed wire.

In this season, my head lights bounce off the walls
of ditchweed,
                    broken and soggy
with winter melt, season of rot and waste,
                                        but I'm lost
in the radio's statistics,
                        two hundred thousand birds,
lost in the grebe's cries
coming through the speakers, the description of the otter,
a pimple in the sea of oil,
                        dead baby on her back.

Wasn't allowed to drive a car,
                    but they let him pilot a single-hulled ship,

Chuck says, when the news of Hazelwood's DUI
sweeps through the fine metal screen of the radio's speakers.

A car lurches into the villa parking lot,
smoke curling from its tailpipe,
reminding me of the twenty-nozzle DDT sprayer
my mother pulled behind the John Deere
through the county's cotton, liquid funneling out
like storm clouds. A cardboard box sign
fills his back window, scrawled over with the words:
                              BOYCOTT EXXON
and I do

though Big Mike says it's all the same gas, says he's seen
the tankers supply Chevron, Shell, Exxon, same truck
at every station. I don't know if I should believe him:
he's a man desperate for attention, needful of lies,

                                       only days out of jail

for rape, a fourteen-year-old,
a girl half his age, though he'll have me know
    he wasn't the first
               or the oldest.

The cost of civilization, Exxon's P.R. man says,
and I limp to my truck with a turkey sub
for a hungry frat boy three miles away
                   and peel off in a bedlam of horns and exhaust.

Judy Jordan

Surrender in the Twentieth Year of My Mother's Death

On the phone, voice traveling the miles of clay fields
to these rock clutches of hopeful rhododendron,
my brother insists I take her home with me, this ghost
he's convinced is our mother. Funny how the dead can't stop
stumbling through our lives. Even after twenty years,
she comes to him every day, blocking doorways, face floating
in the mirror beside his lathered one, razor trembling in his fist.

I imagine this, the three hundred miles, air smelling of snuff,
then lint and the clean of fresh-picked cotton, then the shuffled-
through-hickory-nut-and-dead-leaves smell, that woods-rot so rich,
so future-full, I want to drop to my knees and dig like a star-mouthed
        mole.

But my brother's furious, wants this ghost out of his house.
Though I tell him she's not our mother but some stray,
somebody else's mother, confused, hungry, hair grown straggly
and gray; he says it again, *come get her*, and I imagine her sitting
rigid beside me in the pick-up all the long miles, then pacing,
bedding plant to bedding plant, rubber skim of her fuzzy pink
        bedroom slippers
across the hose-wet greenhouse floor. But how to imagine that day,

the broken teeth clamoring from my stomach's pit with their constant
knowledge of how it will come at last, day when she turns away,
storm door slamming, her receding back caught in the cataracted
plastic, electric shock of that thrumming toward my brain
which rocks there on its bone-strewn salty shore.

                                               And I tell my brother,
fourth boy meant to be a girl, the mistake, that maybe she means
to make amends, as if unfinished business, words left unsaid,
keeps her hovering at room's edge, worrying
about him, wondering who would remind him to brush
the cockleburs from his eyebrows, who would cook
his daily ration of cotton seed and 'possum, smothered
in sweet potatoes, ghost-face with its human
hands. I remember how it looked so much like his pet beagle,
mama had to beat him before he'd eat it.

He remembers that we did eat my pet rooster,
red banty with black wings I spent hours calling
for from the field's edge, not knowing what was cut
into the dumpling stew and I feel my heart shudder
as a lens of desire somewhere deep inside me opens;
who, I wonder, is going to remember my pink-eye
medicine, the ring worm salve, who will bake me birthday
cakes of layered eyeteeth and rose petals?

Look at me here, I cry out to the mottled clouds
stitching and unstitching above the thrashing trees,
living in a greenhouse, naked, with my water hose showers
and boiling cook pot of cumin seeds and butterfly wings,
waving a red flag of surrender, running lost
and wild through the fields of Longhorn bulls.

Autumn

Finally it happens. Giving up, I become the daisy.
Near weed, straggling hairy-stemmed from the poorest
dirt into the smallest hint of sun. Black-eyed Susan.

Brown eye with its ring of yellow teeth.

Sun's eye in waste fields, at the bad-luck crossroads,
beside every chip and gravel street like hungry runaway girls
wearing their frilly yellow skirts, smoking
to stave away the stomach's rumblings.

The Sanskrit word for tree
is *Padapa*, one who drinks with her feet.
My feet are tangled with beer cans, used condoms,
broken bottles, and rust-riddled car bumpers.

In Chinese calligraphy two trees make a forest.
Autumn is tree on fire.

Autumn, all the crows following the soldiers into battle,
all the birds beating their wings against the cut edge of the glass sky,
and I push my seedy head into the most prim flower beds.

Pada-popagata is Sanskrit for abiding under a tree while expecting death.

The children come with their clammy hands
to twist my throat, to drown me in aspirin and sugar water.
They want to make peace with the long-legged giants
crashing through the kitchen each morning.

Let's hope they can find their own way home,
that they don't get lost in the woods again.

Prometheus Comforts Io

This spring the world was awash in wild onions
but flowers will not bloom here again, nor air
smell like spiced lemons or trees
fill with fire and release pink seeds to the sky.

Bathe in steam, bathe in water from the hose, sleep
with frogs bumping all night under your bed, become someone else
somersaulting through the steel of the star-struck night.
Listen to the trees sway in wind; the sound just under the sound.

Smell the soil, ripeness of rot, breath of all living creatures.
Sense the sensuous. Become a shaman. Ask the plants the secret
to the universe. There it is in its wooden box.

Let the alien gaze strip you naked; grow hooves, grow feathers,
spin silk, grow hungry. No. Hungrier. Prepare to shape-change.

Join the chatter and swirl of cicadas as they claw
from their seventeen-year death. Feel in your body the creek
choked in run-off, death idling his bulldozer.

Now it sleeps this world it sleeps it sleeps now it sleeps.

Rachel's Tail

Y̶ou never want to piss off a girl named Rachel Goldblatt, especially if she has a knee-length tail covered in fur.

Now, I know you're thinkin', "Oh come on, we've read those medical reports and heard they find them one in every million babies or so. But they snip that tiny thing off at the same time as the umbilical and it never grows back."

Except this time it did.

Nearly 20 years ago, as Doctor Mulroney was around front, detaching Rachel from her mother, Nurse Phillips took three snapshots with her Kodak and then watched as the aging pediatrician lopped off the baby's half-inch tail. Six months later, he clipped it again when the anomaly, as he called it, had poked out to almost an inch and a quarter. And just prior to the girl's second birthday, with the now finely furred tail long enough to protrude from her panties, the doctor gave in and convinced her parents that it was God's desire to just let it grow.

When the appendage was almost as thick as her father's thumb, at age three and a half, it was over 30 inches long. Rachel's mother wrapped it around her child's waist, thus hiding it with stretch-elastic pants and forbid the girl to play with it in public. Those friends and relatives who knew of the tail's existence never spoke of it, lest someone might be a close confidante of the family and cause unneeded embarrassment. None of the other children at family gatherings admitted to touching it, although it's a sure bet they did.

Her mother, though, couldn't keep her hands off it.

Jewish to the extent that she and her husband had only had sex once and that through a hole in the bed sheet as proscribed by the ancients. Her mother saw the tail as absolute proof of God's existence. During her diaper years, Rachel was changed so often that the owner of the delivery service assigned them a dedicated driver and truck. Her mother said the finger of the Almighty touched her baby's tail. Her father said it was a Jewish rabbit's foot. At the age of three, Rachel began to wonder what all the fuss was about.

During the spring of 1968, prior to the end of Rachel's first year in kindergarten, her mother heard a call from the heavens to go west. God came to the woman in a fit of sneezing brought on by the spoonful of red-hot horseradish the child had splattered in her mother's face. It would be the last helping of Sunday morning gefilte fish they would consume.

The image of God appeared to her mother in the guise of George Washington, identical to the first president's face on a one-dollar bill. Geographically challenged, the woman interpreted the vision to mean Mount Rushmore and the wisdom of the old cherry-picker, but she couldn't remember if it was on the north or south side of the Dakotas. Rachel, who'd gulped down several glasses of water in an attempt to quench the forest fire in her throat, belched out something that sounded like "north" and thus the question was answered.

A month later, the family sold their Chicago apartment and purchased a two hundred acre cattle ranch in Balta, North Dakota. The nearest deli was a six-hour drive, the synagogue was an overnight trip, and the Yellow Pages were a pair of index cards the former owner had tacked next to the telephone. Rachel stood in the gravel driveway and cried until long after the first sunset before her mother dragged her into the house, making the child stand naked in her bedroom until she collapsed.

That evening, Rachel and God parted ways.

Now her father, whose name is superfluous, since he doesn't survive the first winter without a landlord to maintain the furnace, knew less about cattle than he did about log fires. But he did enjoy a good porterhouse, and figured he'd bought enough cows to last a lifetime. Mother Goldblatt, who refused to answer to any other name, followed her husband into the good earth the following year. She was a vegetarian.

Rachel was left to the care of a weathered ranch hand named Flop and his wife, Frederica, whom everyone referred to as Freddy. The couple, childless due to one too many hard bounces on the saddle for Flop, were proficient in raising bovines but clueless when it came to children. Having more faith in the Lord than themselves, they brought the six-year-old to the Catholic mission serving the Sioux Indian reservation, a half a day's ride south of the ranch.

Father Sicola, who by virtue of his name would never be a candidate for Pope, was at first reviled by the sight of the tail. Easily swayed by a bribe, he agreed to allow Rachel's schooling after Flop offered him one cow per semester, butchered and delivered. However, when they completed the registration forms using her surname, the priest fell backward out of his chair.

"She's Jewish?" He snatched the jeweled crucifix hanging from his neck and held it between him and the tainted paper.

Freddy wrapped her arms around the girl. "She's so far from her God right now that maybe the old religion just faded away and she's clean as fresh snow."

Father Sicola let the cross drop back against his flannel shirt and lifted the chair from the floor. "But what about *that*?" He pointed at Rachel's tail, the tip popping up from the top of her sweatpants. "How do I explain that to the rest of the school?"

As he donned his grease-stained nine-gallon hat, Flop smiled at the priest and said, "Tell 'em that her mom was a fox and her daddy was a bear. As a girl, she gets her genes from mom's side of the family and I wouldn't mess with her, if they was smart." He winked at the priest. "She gonna be tough one. Kick up some serious dust, even in a windstorm."

The priest genuflected and put his hand on the girl's head. "Pray St. Germanicus protects you from the two-legged beasts that await you."

Rachel just shrugged and tucked the tail back into her pants.

On the first day of school, Father Sicola walked his newest student from the mission's dormitory to the schoolhouse before any of the other children arrived. He sat the girl at a desk alongside his podium, facing the classroom.

As his students, all Sioux ranging in age from six years to fifteen, marched, strode, and stumbled into the one-room schoolhouse, they stood behind their desks, waiting for his command.

"Ladies and gentlemen, please be seated." The priest shoved his hands in the back pockets of his dungarees and sauntered around to the front row of children, the youngest. "We have several new students this fall." As he read the stick-on nametags of the two boys and one girl seated to his right, each child stood and faced the class, which applauded, before the student returned to his or her seat.

Father Sicola stepped back and put his hand on Rachel's shoulder. "This is Rachel, she's also new to the school, but she does not come from the reservation."

Following the example of the others, Rachel slid out of the chair and took a confident step forward. Uncomfortable with its position, she had pulled the tail out of her pants, behind her, letting it drop casually to her thighs. When she turned to retake her seat, the furry appendage swished across the desktops of two of the children in the front row.

The girl, one of the newcomers and the same age as Rachel, screamed as the tip of the tail knocked her pencil box to the floor.

The boy, seven years old and in his second year at the mission's school, reached out and grabbed on, pulling Rachel toward him as he howled, "*Sungina, sungina*, I have the fox by the tail!"

"Let her go!" the priest shrieked, slamming the boy's wrist with a yardstick. "How would you feel if I grabbed your, your," he stuttered, "your hair and yanked like that?"

The boy dropped Rachel's tail, quickly covering his crotch with his hands.

Rachel spun on her heels and punched the boy in the nose.

Over the next seven years, tailed and tailless skirmished several times as new children were introduced to the girl and succumbed to the temptation to know the truth. Those who were older than Rachel performed the ritual on a dare and surreptitiously touched the hairy curlicue the first chance they got; the younger ones simply asked to touch it, usually after they had the tip of it already in their hands. Word of the *Wikoska Yamni Hu*—girl with three legs—spread across the reservation, and the customary visit of the mother of a Sioux child on the first day of classes at the mission expanded to include aunts and uncles anxious for a peek.

Father Sicola allowed the elders of the tribe to see the child firsthand, having convinced Rachel not to bloody their bulbous noses when they fondled her tail. They returned to their compounds spouting legends of the daughter of the fox and bear who had taken the tail of the fox, but the face of the bear, and an ugly one at that.

As Rachel grew into a teenager, the tail stabilized at her knees. Covered with the same oak colored hair as her ponytail, she had abandoned all hope of disguising her *yamni hu* and was content to let it all hang out. Even when riding a horse or working summers on the now sprawling family ranch, the girl wore a skirt; and for comfort's sake—the shorter the better.

No one in the tribe rode sidesaddle. Probably no one in the tribe had ever heard the term. Girls sat on a horse the same as boys, urged the horse across the rocky desert with the same spirit of freedom. Boys had leather underwear. Girls had cotton. With her tail flying in the wind behind her, Rachel's first equine orgasm ended with a scream that frightened coyotes in both Dakotas. In that moment of blissful awakening, everything evil she'd heard about sex from the gaggle of nuns at the mission lost credibility. If it was this good on a horse, it had to be earth shattering with a boy.

Unfortunately, the misfortune of her familial genes—father's flat cheekbones and mother's pug nose—bore out Flop's prediction in grand style. While it wasn't a bear's face, it was neither that of magazine cover girl. The boys who shunned Rachel in the hope of bedding a cheerleader or some local beauty were of as little interest to her as she was to them. However, the toughs in the tribe—boys who would accept her challenge to wrestle or really run their hardest when she would race them—ignited her curiosity. With strength came virility, even if it dulled the intellect.

The choices seemed myriad at first; these were not frumpy, educated types her family had left behind in Chicago. These were Sioux—proud, tough, one generation north of the loincloths in the winter. However, as a white girl in the closed society of the Sioux, with or without a tail, the selection of screwable men was limited. Add to that the horrific downpour of hellfire and brimstone they all endured at the mission and Rachel was having little success at getting her dates to unzip their jeans.

Buck Steelfeather, at 19, had the marbled muscles of a quarry worker, ran on the feet of a deer, but was stumped by the difference between mashed and baked on the diner's menu.

With the waitress tapping her pencil on the edge of her glasses, the tail swished under the table and poked Buck in the groin, something it taken to doing on its own lately. Rachel yanked it back, sat on it, and grit her teeth. "She's not asking who you'd vote for in the

Tribal Council, shit for brains, just a side dish to go with your hamburger."

"Shoot, I'll just have 'em fried then." He folded the menu shut and handed it to the waitress, waiting until she walked back to the counter and asked. "Whatta you mean, 'ain't I done it yet?' Done what?"

Rachel's eyes rolled up to stare at a brown water stain on a ceiling tile directly over her head. Scolding him in voice coated in ice, she spoke just loud enough for the three men at the counter to turn their heads, "Had sex, you idiot. Screwed a squaw. Rode the mustang bareback. For God's sake..."

"Don't you use the Lord's name in vain. Father Sicola will..."

"Father Sicola will do what? Roll his four hundred pound ass out of that cushy leather chair and vapor-lock as he tries to run over here and chastise me?" Rachel slapped her hand on the table and sneered. "His God is waiting for him to wheeze up through the pearly gates just to laugh at him."

Buck sat back hard in his side of the booth, holding the table with both hands. "After all these years, and all his teachings, are you saying you don't believe in God?"

Rachel leaned in and pointed at her nose. "With a face like this?" She grabbed her tail and laid a foot of it on her napkin in between the fork and knife. "And this? You expect me to believe in God? Come on, Buck, am I the work of a serious, all-knowing, all-powerful, white robed deity?"

The boy scratched his head. "What's a deity?"

Two hours later, in the back of his father's station wagon, Rachel had him screaming the names of the Apostles, as she sat on his knees with her tail wrapped around his jewels. Sadly, the elder Steelfeather, hearing the commotion, yanked open the car door before she had a chance to mount him and dragged her out by the hair.

Her next challenge was three months her junior, but had entered the mission's program only two years ago. William Clearsky was the one boy who had no fear challenging Rachel to a race. He'd beaten her to and from the creek three times and even with a five-count head start, she couldn't outrace him from the mission to the highway—barely a hundred yards in the dust.

Almost a head taller than the girl, he had to duck to enter most doorways. Much to the enjoyment of the other boys, the doorframe over the mission's classroom had collided with his head several times since his arrival. Rachel wondered if the rest of his body held to the same oversized proportions as his legs and was determined to find out.

It took her several attempts, but William finally agreed to a date at the drive-in movie theater, but only if they each paid their way. Rachel consented to the silly rule, but insisted that he let *her* buy the popcorn and sodas.

Halfway through the coming attractions, she let her hand slip from the popcorn container and into his lap. William quickly lifted it by her fingers and placed the hand back on the girl's knee.

"Don't you like to be touched there?" she asked him.

"I guess," he replied, "but I've never had a girl do it."

Rachel slid away from him on the bench seat, stopping against the passenger door. "You let other boys touch it?"

"No." William's head drooped as he spoke toward his knees. "I'm the only one who's ever touched it before."

The tail squirmed underneath her, but Rachel had wrapped a loop of the seat belt around it. William knew about the now famous tail but had yet to see it for himself. He could have all the tail he wanted when they were finished.

Relieved, she shoved herself back to his side, smiling. "Well, then it's time you let someone else give it a tug."

"I can't." He shook his head and laid his hands in his lap.

"You can't what?"

"I promised Father Sicola I would wait until I got married." William rolled down the window and unhooked the speaker box. He got out of the car and slammed the door.

"Where are you going?"

"I...I...I have to go to the men's room." He stumbled away from the car. "I'll be right back."

Rachel finished her soda and started on his. She watched the movie alone when he failed to return and walked home with half the popcorn when it was over. William never spoke to her again.

On her eighteenth birthday—a Saturday night—Rachel hitched a ride with two other girls from the school into Bismarck. During the three-hour drive, most of the conversation was about getting off the 'res' and out into the world. Rachel asked both of them if they'd ever been in bed with a boy. One of them said she'd slept with her cousin on a visit to Fargo, but only because her sister had taken the smaller bed. The other one grimaced and asked if she was serious or not.

They split up upon reaching the city, Rachel telling them not worry, she'd get a ride back one way or another. As the two girls marched off in search of a department store, she pushed the tail down from her waist and out the back of her skirt.

Sounds of a rock and roll band drifted out the open doors of a bar drawing the teen toward them. A bouncer stood across the opening, watching the band rehearse while he gulped a can of soda. Rachel tried to squeeze around him, but the man stopped her with a massive hand on her shoulder.

"Where do you think you're going?"

"I heard the music and thought I'd…"

"Thought you'd what? Bring your underage ass into this bar and get us all locked up?" The bouncer turned Rachel around. "Go on over to the diner and drop some quarters in the jukebox. You can come back here when you're old enough."

As she began to dig in her pocketbook for the driver's license Flop had taken her to get last weekend, her tail flipped angrily against the man's knees.

"What the?" He inched backward from the girl, crossing himself as he went. "Goodnight Irene; please tell me that thing isn't real!"

Rachel paused her search, looked down at the tail, and sighed. "Yes it's real. I've had it my entire life." She found the wallet and tugged out the driver's license. "My entire eighteen years."

The bouncer took the laminated ID card and scanned it with one glance, returning his eyes to Rachel's legs and the furry probe sticking out between them.

"It's not a costume?"

"No. It's permanently attached." She snatched the license from his hands. "Can I come in now?"

Just then, a ragged hair boy in jeans and a white shirt pushed the bouncer aside, flicking his cigarette into the gutter. Before she could say a word, the boy lifted the license from her fingers and read her name, "Rachel Goldblatt. Jewish?"

She snatched the license from his hand and stuffed it back into her pocketbook. "So? You've never seen a Jewish girl?"

21

He shook his head. "Not in these parts. Mostly Sioux and drunken locals." He squinted as he looked at Rachel's face, before pulling a pair of wire-rimmed glasses from his pocket. Making a closer inspection, now with her in focus, the boy started at her face and worked his way down her flowered shirt to her waist and short leather skirt. The tail brought his appraisal to an abrupt halt.

"Very cool. It looks so real." The boy looked at the date on his watch. "Isn't Halloween a few months away?"

Rachel closed her pocketbook and tightened her fist. "Are you two idiots brothers?"

The boy sized up the bouncer and shook his head. "Nah, he's too ugly to be my brother. Jake, why is this girl standing out here on the sidewalk…wagging her tail in the breeze?"

With a shrug, the bouncer stepped clear of the doorway and ushered Rachel into the bar.

His name was Christian, lead guitarist for a country-western band that had as much hope of fame as any of the hundreds of other bands slogging across the Midwest that summer. While the rest of the musicians argued over a change in the set list for that evening's performance, Christian got two cold beers from the bartender and guided Rachel to an empty table.

She lifted the tail and placed it into his hands. "Everyone asks to touch it. Go ahead, get it over with."

Stroking the tip with his index finger and thumb as if judging the quality of a piece of fabric, Christian worked his fingers slowly up the proffered length of fur. The tail stiffened; the top half of it straight enough to hold a flag. He blinked in disbelief. "It's been there your entire life?"

Rachel nodded.

"All Jewish girls have one?"

"Are you really that ignorant?"

She started to get up from the chair, but he put his hand on her wrist and held her back. "No. I'm just kidding you. But, honestly, I've never met a Jewish girl before."

"Never been East?"

"Nope. But I've got a bunch of postcards from Milwaukee."

Rachel took her tail out his hand and slipped it behind her.

"What do you do with it when you…" He smiled. "…have sex?"

The clatter of a falling cymbal startled her. She waited until the drummer had shouted "Sorry!" before admitting, "I haven't yet."

"Ah, so you've come to the big city to find the answer."

Another nod.

Christian called over to his band mates, "Are we done?" An assortment of affirmatives was the reply. He chugged the beer and checked his watch. "We've got a few hours until show time. Let's go for a walk."

The stroll was brief, two blocks south, one east, through a hotel lobby and down a carpeted hallway to his room. The sex was even faster, not exactly what Rachel had hoped for on her first time, but it answered all the questions—hers *and* his.

The tail was an eleventh finger, caressing his legs while she worked down from his neck to his waist. He giggled and curled his toes as it swished against them, kicking it from foot to foot, much to her annoyance.

"You wouldn't want me to play pinball with your nuts would you?"

"I'm ticklish!" he protested.

She straddled his waist, putting the furry rope in his hand. "Then it's best you hold onto this until we're done." Rachel grinned. "Sometimes it has a mind of its own."

And when they were finished, sitting side by side on the rumpled bed sheets, Christian asked her, "Well, was it what you expected?"

Rachel blushed. "I'm not sure, but I liked it. It's definitely better than a horse." She turned to face him. "What about you?"

He pulled a towel over his naked waist and shrugged. "I've never been to bed with a Jewish girl before. But if they've all got tails like yours, I'd be more than happy to try another one."

Rachel groaned and punched him in the nose.

In The Land of Children

Exiting the train one rainy afternoon in Berlin, I was approached in the station by one solitary boy, no more than five years old. "English," he asked. "English?" The rest of the crowd forked around him, but I found it much harder to ignore hazel colored eyes that peeked through shaggy black bangs, looking hopefully from me to his outstretched, stained palms. "English?"

I nodded.

His eyes darkened. "Gimme your money," he spat. "I said gimme your money!" He stepped forward, so close I could see the black decay creeping its way down his gums festering deep into his graying baby teeth. "This is a stick-up."

I stared at him, then looked for his backup. There was no one around but passing commuters speeding on and off trains, not acknowledging the boy. I wanted to take him home and clean the black from under his fingernails. I wanted to make him oatmeal with milk and sprinkled cinnamon. I wanted to sit him down and teach him the ways my language could be used for poetry, not just aggression. But I reached into my pocket and tossed him a two-euro coin. He clenched it in his fist and faded into the crowd singing in the language he had learned, "English? English?"

I walked from the station with legs that betrayed my strength. There was no real danger with the boy, only the knowledge that his mother had taught him ways of the street, the words "money" and "stick-up", the dark shames of a desperate adulthood reached far too soon.

Or perhaps she was teaching him the only way she knew to survive.

Just then, commotion rose from the crowd as the boy dashed with his mother, her skirt flapping wildly, out of the train station with two officers at quick clip behind them. As the mother saw the yellow tram hurdling toward them, she pushed her son to the other side of the tracks. At the last moment of safety, she jumped with him, separated from the officers by that yellow streak of train on grinding metal. She seemed to know they only needed those few moments to escape the handcuff's clutches, and as they ran down the street, weaving through crowds of gawking tourists, the boy's laughter reeled high and excited, as if he had won something in this life of escape.

When the wall came down, Berlin was flooded with foreigners. It was a complex system of immigration, allowing some to transition easily, while others were condemned to years of red tape, or worse, deportation. Some fought the system while others simply slipped into the shadows, hoping that even the darkness would provide a brighter future for their children. When I came to the city as an American nanny, I was met by parks full of children with nappy red afros, soft blonde curls, or hair stick-straight as black licorice. I lived in *Prinzlauer Berg*—which locals jokingly referred to as "The Land of Children"—a neighborhood with more parks per square meter than any other city in the world. From my balcony I saw the constant flow of families walking to and from the parks, children wound onto their mothers' backs with lengths of colored fabric, children straddling seats screwed into the handlebars of their parents' bicycles, children—up to fifteen at a time—perched in wooden carriages pulled like rickshaws behind the bicycles of daycare workers, steady legs chugging.

The Danish family I worked for enrolled their three-year-old daughter, Nala, into an English and German speaking preschool, hoping she would acquire three fluent tongues. In the mornings, I arrived at seven to change Nala for school. I picked up her slumbering infant brother, just weeks old, and rested him against my chest, winding yards of green fabric around us, encapsulating him in a makeshift womb. Some days, Nala's mother joined us, accent lilting through conversations like the waves of the Baltic Sea. She strained with the healing of a body that had just birthed her son, some days sweaty and aching as she leaned over wooden crates of grapefruits, bitter radishes, and salted peanuts at the neighborhood market. She rolled gooseberries between her fingers, squeezed pomegranates, and brought round cantaloupes to her nose. Behind the counter, an old Asian man with wrinkles spider-webbed across his face watched us anxiously, nodding encouragements as we picked through the mountain of apricots we would take home to slice, carefully removing each pit, so Nala could snack, fingers turned sticky from the juice.

On days like this, we strolled through the neighborhood stopping to buy freshly cut Stargazer lilies, or to sip tiny ceramic cups of cappuccino. Some days, we sat chewing cherries at the corner side bistro, piling pits like anthills, our fingers stained red as brick walls. It was on a day like that, with the baby nestled safely in his mother's chest, that a gypsy woman wearing a flowing yellow skirt thrust a piece of paper into our hands.

"English?" she pleaded. "English?"

The note she handed us was scrawled with chicken-scratch letters, as though copied from a child's spelling book, all capitals, screaming off the page: HUNGRY BABY AT HOME. PLEASE HELP.

These gypsy women prowl the neighborhoods in Berlin, sometimes selling their wares, sometimes not. Always, it seems, begging. Sometimes the women sit cross-legged at stations, Mohawked babies resting in the cradle between their folded knees, inky eyes shrouded under long, elegant scarves, hands outstretched, crooning, *Bitte. Bitte.* Please. When women like this are lucky, someone running to catch a commuting train would see the baby shake his arm, jingling the bells tied with rope to his wrist, and drop a euro coin into the mother's palm. But when she approached us at the bistro table, we shook our heads, passed back the note, and whispered our apologies as she turned away, skirt dancing like wind sweeping sand in some faraway desert.

The morning after the train station stick up, I returned to Nala's house and made her the same breakfast I had dreamed of making the boy: oatmeal with warm milk and sprinkled cinnamon. While she spooned the breakfast sloppily into her mouth, I couldn't help but think of the boy, wondering who made sure his fingernails were clean, and who made sure his belly was full.

Later, I sat for two hours at the park as Nala raked her fingers in long paths through the sand, filled buckets with water, and mixed it together into patties she pretended to bake. When the sun drooped behind the trees we made our way from the park to the grocer. I nodded to that old Asian man who greeted me as a friend, wrinkling smiles with his eyes. He reached an ancient, yellowing hand to lead Nala, with her pattered steps, to the apricots mounded haphazardly on a splintered wooden table.

As I reached to thumb avocadoes and Fuji apples, searching for freshness, laughter swooped behind me. Thinking a rickshaw of children might be hurtling down the sidewalk, I pressed my body against the crates, protecting the baby. But instead of a distracted daycare worker pedaling toward us, I saw three small Asian children, wearing white tank tops faded grey and bicycle shorts as tattered as if they had spent a lifetime battling monsoon winds. The children grabbed handfuls of globe grapes, stuffing pockets like hamster cheeks, before the owner batted them away. They leapt from the sidewalk as quickly as they arrived, disappearing behind a green minivan's sliding door. The old man looked from the parked van to me with eyes wide as a cornered animal's. It did not take much else for me to realize these children belonged to him, and as he rubbed the worried wrinkles at his temples, I knew I was not meant to see what he had hidden.

As the summer progressed, I passed the man's shop each morning as I took Nala, her tiny fingers laced through mine, to preschool and back home again. I was never able to tear my eyes from the green minivan parked along the curbside next to the crates of blood oranges and pineapples. There were moments when I saw the dark silhouettes of heads in movement like dancing, and others when they sat completely still, as frightened deer, waiting for the danger to pass. I imagined the children stealing handfuls of mangoes, strawberries, walnuts, before climbing back into the safety of the van, just as I imagined the gypsy boy stacking euro coins into towers balanced, clinking onto his palm. And I hoped at night, when the officers had long since gone to sleep, that the children could escape their confines to play in the neighborhood we shared, overrun with parks they must have stared at in longing while trapped by their parent's choices. Neither here nor really there. In this city they are like shadows, locked away in the land of children, hiding.

Looking For Ghosts

Dawn's pink fingers unfold lavender
Skies—shades of Spring before she arrives.

Another day begins. Are you alone
wherever you're waking up?

Gray fox slips through mist, black tips of fur
a shock of dark in white fog.

Rain blusters into the afternoon, reduces
light to greenish glow. *Days like this*

we went back to bed—cheek and shoulder
caressing—savoring the patter outside.

Rivers rise, gnaw the banks, tentacles
of fear invading the field, the street, the yard.

Dusk drizzles into a wet whisper. Buds crushed,
puddles pour frogs, turtles trench the mud.

Remember getting stuck in the woods—traction lost
in mire and leaves, gaping ruts landing

us in the truck bed watching the sky
grow bright with stars? The river retreats,

vines and trash tangled in streets as lights blink
on, and mist smears the darkening night.

Rich Murphy

Perpetual Peace and Mississippi

Only the dismemberment of its Trinity
brought peace to Faulkner's South. Black
shadows of the cross haunt the poem
of tree and forest. The loneliest man in

American literature loses himself between
parental black ram and white ewe. If it
weren't the forsaken Joe Christmas, another
scapegoat would adorn the foot of a European

hierarchy. (The North doesn't get away
with its autopsy of its victim either. Atlanta
laid drawn and quartered.) The Magi,
distracted from a lynching's orgasm, bond

into family of wish and hope ever after
while the next need to neglect then blame
emerges from the readers' uteri. The ends
of wires face each other without an art for life.

Where We Come From

Kiev, Russia, Early 1900's

Max didn't know that it would be the last time they'd be together. How could he? Even though he was a child, and they tried to protect him, he knew something bad was going on. Everyone who came and went over the past week whispered, looking over at the children cautiously, nervously. But he never expected what happened that evening, it was beyond his worst imagining. Mother had just finished cleaning the kitchen. She made chicken soup for dinner and the house still had the salty, savory smell that lingered warmly in the air. He was looking forward to the leftovers on the following day. There was supposed to be a next day.

Philadelphia, 1964

They lived on the corner in a simple, brick row house. Your mother dropped you off at the driveway, and you walked up the four cement steps that lead from the street to the small little slab of porch where their green metal chairs sat unused. You looked up at the bay window expecting to see your grandmother's face, but she wasn't looking out impatiently awaiting your arrival as she once would. The tweedy beige curtains hung unremarkably, closed almost all the way except for a slit where darkened light emanated. You were twelve years old and it was your job to help them on Fridays after school. Your grandfather always rewarded you for your efforts with a trinket or some pocket change. He still had drawers full of little calendars, some with magnets on the back, and all sorts of key chains from the food distributors that used to service his grocery store. You now had a drawer full yourself. The grocery store had been in the old neighborhood and was known as the Jewish market back when the neighborhood had been different. Before hostile neighbors moved in and did everything in their power to claim the territory as their own. It was odd how people acted back then. People of different colors and religions bonded together in their common hate until life had actually become dangerous for the few Jews who remained.

Your grandfather didn't talk about that though. He talked about all the little things he brought home to your grandmother. He used to laugh and tease her about what she did with the trinkets that he brought home. He said she'd find a use for just about anything. Once, he brought home cigarettes that were given to him from a cigarette distributor and your grandmother, he said, naively sat down to smoke the pack, even though she was not a smoker and had never been, because they were free. Grandfather's eyes watered at the memory, laughing softly as he told you. But that was back before the store closed. Nobody mentioned the store anymore, at least not in front of your grandfather. It had been his greatest achievement. He came from nothing, he often said, reminding you that he'd started out sweeping the floors until one day he owned the store.

Your grandmother could never understand why he couldn't just make the money like other people; why he was always giving things away. As they watched the old neighborhood decline, more and more people came to get their groceries on credit. Most of the time they didn't pay it back. But your grandfather still gave them credit the next time they came in. Your grandmother would say, "You're not a rich man, Max," to which he would quietly reply, "They have children, Emma."

Then the burglaries started. In all, your grandfather was robbed at knifepoint three times. One of those times they tied him up and locked him in the freezer. You remember when you went to see him the next day and he wouldn't speak to anyone. Alone, he sat at the dining room table with his prayer cloth and the scroll with the cords wrapped around his sleeve. He prayed continually, rocking and crying. Your grandmother whispered to you that it's called davening. You remember feeling helpless, wishing that someone would get him a tissue and ask him if he was okay. You wanted to reach out and wipe the tears from his face.

Kiev, Russia, Early 1900's

Max helped his little brother, Abe, wash up and get ready for bed while his older sister, Rachel, did the same for Gerda. Gerda was easy. She was only three but wanted to do everything herself. She was always smiling, her dimples deeply denting into her plump rosy cheeks. She looked very much like Abe did when he was her age. Abe was only three years older than Gerda, but was already showing signs of being very smart. He could read almost as well the older two and he talked constantly. Max could barely get a word out to answer before the next question was being flung at him. Abe would pull on Max's sleeve eagerly with small jerking movements to hurry the answers. And then there was Rachel, who was so much like their father, stern but soft, understanding but impatient. All the children had dark hair and everyone in the family had hazel eyes, except for Gerda and Max. They had deep brown eyes, almost black. Gerda would rub and rub at her sleepy brown eyes with one hand, and the other, at least the thumb, was always in her mouth.

Mother and Father were sitting at the dining room table drinking hot tea and talking quietly while the children sat on their parent's bed warm and soft in their night clothes. Max began reading from the Torah. They were reading Exodus, picking up where they'd left off the night before. He'd just finished reading about Moses coming down from the mountain when they heard a hard banging on the door.

Philadelphia, 1964

On that particular Friday it was biting cold. When you stepped into the front room you still felt cold. Your grandma was asleep in her oversized yellow chair. The T.V. was on but turned down to a low hum. Your grandfather patted your cheeks softly with the warm palms of his hands as you unbuttoned your coat.

"Do you want me to wash the dishes?" you asked, picking up some stray glasses and carrying them to the kitchen.

Grandpa waved this away with his fingertips and then gently pushed you toward a chair at the kitchen table.

"First, we warm you up."

You decided that the floors needed to be washed as he made you a cup of hot tea. He apologized for being out of sugar and bent his head away from you. You were quick to tell him that you didn't really like sugar in your tea. He rested his hand on the top of your head and smiled, telling you with his shiny eyes that he knew you better than that.

There was a dull thud in the front room. You hurried out to find that your grandma had knocked her teacup off the table. She was still asleep, her mouth slightly open. You loved that their living room always had a warm woody scent to it, like wood that had been sitting in the sun.

Your grandfather moved slowly, carefully. Even before he was really old he always seemed old. He was built small and was a quiet, gentle man. What made him stand out was the depth of his sad brown eyes. Some people wouldn't even notice him unless he was looking at them. He cleaned up the spilt tea from the dense, wooly carpet and carried your grandmother's cup to the kitchen. He moved like he was carrying something so fragile and precious that it required both hands and his deep concentration. You noticed that your grandmother was now awake and watching him with a tired, detached look.

"Max?" she whispered, appearing confused. And then she suddenly looked over at you and her face came alive with her smile.

"Mama-shayna." She liked to call you that. Her good arm reached out for you and you quickly went to embrace her. She smelled like warm, sleepy staleness and Pond's cold cream.

Max called from the kitchen, "I'll be back in minute. You two be okay?"

You helped her to the bedroom. It used to be the dining room but then all the uncles came and turned it into a bedroom. It was a lot smaller than their old bedroom upstairs. It was strange for you to come over now and not be able to go upstairs; not that their tenant, Mrs. Rosenbach, didn't invite you up. She did, but your grandmother said not to bother her, so you always smiled politely and gave an excuse. Mrs. Rosenbach stopped asking eventually.

Your grandmother turned slightly, and as you held her walker steady she made her way into a sitting position on the bed. She eased herself back against the pillows as you held her outstretched hand.

"Resh-tick-a-far-meerrrr," she groaned as she tried to get her body to cooperate. Ever since the stroke she'd go back and forth from Russian to English to Yiddish, many times in the same sentence. She kept a hold of your hand and closed her eyes. You pulled the quilt up to her soft middle with your free arm. Her face looked full, especially around her eyes, and even though she lay as if asleep there was a smile on her face.

You said, "I love you grandma."

She smiled even bigger. "Thank God for you my Leigh-ala. You always try the best."

"Do you need me to do anything?" you asked.

Her eyes opened in her squinty-smiling way. "I ought to do," she said, pointing with her good arm to her eyebrows while making a plucking motion with her thumb and pointer finger.

You love your grandmother so you try to look happy.

Kiev, Russia, Early 1900's

The children's heads turned toward the sound of the banging. Through the bedroom door, Max could see his parents looking at one another but neither moved to answer. The banging began again this time accompanied by loud, impatient voices. And then his mother was running into the bedroom grabbing the little ones and pulling them to her.

"Mother…" Max started to ask, but she held her hand up with a panicked look that told him to stop.

Her forehead was severely drawn and her eyes seemed to dart from one face to another as she whispered to the little ones not to make a sound. Then their mother carefully but hurriedly pushed them under the bed. The banging continued. The door sounded as if it would collapse in from the weight of the shouting as much as from the banging.

Mother now had Rachel by the arm, as she looked frantically around the bedroom. "Mother," Rachel whispered, "I can fit."

Mother ran her hand down the top of Rachel's head over her long brown hair until it rested on the side of her face. And then Rachel was on the floor trying to get as flat as possible as she squeezed under the bed with Gerda and Abe.

"SShhh," Rachel whispered from under the bed as Gerda began to whine.

The banging came again followed by angry voices. Max wanted to go to his father but his mother was pushing him toward the closet. There was a loud cracking sound followed by a crash, followed by his father's cries. His mother used one arm to pull him behind her as she turned and braced herself for whatever was coming. Max tried to see around her into the front room but she was pressing him so close that her shawl was covering his face. He could hear his father speaking fast, begging mercy.

Max peered around his mother's thick frame and saw several of the Russian secret police. Some were moving about the room knocking over their things while two towered over his father with grim faces. One of them reached forward and took the spectacles from his father's face and snapped them in half. Max strained to get away from his mother but her nails dug firm into his arm.

Philadelphia, 1964

Your grandfather said, "Look what I have for you," closing the back door and then holding out a bag of fresh pastries.

You turned from the stove where you were finishing scrubbing the range top. He stepped forward but then jumped back realizing that you'd washed the floors. Using the tip of his right shoe he held down his left heel, slipping his foot out, and then he did the same with his left foot. He walked to the table and set the pastries down and then came to the stove and looked down at it thoughtfully. His eyes began to water.

"What's wrong grandfather?" you asked.

He stepped back and pulled out his handkerchief. It took a minute for the emotion to pass.

"Look how you've worked so hard."

You gave him your most cheerful smile, setting the sponge down and going to hug him. He began to sob, big trembling sobs. He patted you gently on the shoulder and moved away to leave the room. Your eyes filled with warm tears as you watched him leave. You wished that those awful burglars had never robbed your grandfather; they turned him into such a sad man.

When he returned he was holding a white embroidered handkerchief.

"I have something to give you for all this hard work. This was your great-grandmother's. She was the best. There is no one like your great-grandmother, except for maybe my Leigh-ala."

You gave him a kiss on the cheek. "Thank you, grandfather."

Kiev, Russia, Early 1900's

Max's father put his hands together as if in prayer and bowed humbly, his shoulders slumped. There was sweat dripping from his temples. The man who seemed to tower over his father raised his hand stiffly and then brought it down on the side of his father's head. From behind his mother, he watched as his father fell to his knees and reached for his head.

36

Max pulled as hard as he could, pushing his mother as he tore his arm from her grip. "Foter!" Max ran into the front room, his mother screaming behind him.

A fist came out of nowhere striking him square in the face. Max felt his legs give out from under him. He had the urge to reach out and break his fall but couldn't lift his arms. It felt like he was trying to swim through sand. His father leaned over to him, crying, begging the men to stop. Max felt his father's tears dampening his face.

The police were teasing Max's mother, pulling at her clothing. They asked her where the others were hiding.

"Tell us," they said, "and we might let them live."

She didn't say a word. One of them took his gun and tapped it against the palm of his other hand as he walked slowly toward the bedroom.

"Ikh bet dikh, please, I beg you, don't hurt the children," his father cried.

Max's mother backed into the doorway of the bedroom, using her body to block their way. Her eyes were wide and frantic. She shook her head slightly as she placed one hand against the doorframe. In the other hand she held tight to a white handkerchief, holding it out in front of her as if she were surrendering.

Max felt his father's arms around him. He was rocking and praying for God to save them. He heard his mother gasp, and then a gunshot. Max heard the dull thud of something heavy hitting the floor. He tried to open his eyes, but just barely managed the right one. Screams were coming from the bedroom. He thought it was Rachel but he couldn't see. And then he heard another shot, and then another.

His father was sobbing uncontrollably, reaching his arms toward his wife and daughter who lay out of reach. The man who'd hit Max took out his gun and brought it down over his father's head. Max tried to catch him as he crumbled to the floor. The police were all moving into the bedroom now. Max looked down at his father helplessly as he tried to get up into a sitting position. When he wiped the wetness from his brow he realized it was blood but didn't know if it was his or his father's. The doorway to the bedroom seemed far. Max crawled toward the bedroom and pulled himself up against the doorframe. He watched as one of the policemen pulled Gerda out from under the bed by her foot. Gerda was kicking wildly; her little slipper came off her foot in the man's hand. She scrambled back underneath the bed. The man reached more aggressively under the bed but Abe's little arm came jutting out. He began hammering his fist as hard as he could on the man's arm.

Max stumbled into the bedroom trying not to look at his mother and sister. He called out to the men that he would give them whatever they wanted but not to hurt the little ones.

"Please, they're only children."

"And what do you have to give us?" one of them asked. They all laughed at this.

A man with small black eyes came up to him and grabbed him by the back of his pajama shirt jerking him into the center of the room.

"He has nothing."

A different man now had Abe out from under the bed and was standing behind him holding him by the throat. Abe just stared mutely at his mother and sister who lay silent on the floor. Max looked from Abe to the bed. Another man was trying to reach Gerda.

"A brokh!" The man trying to get Gerda yelled as he jumped back holding his hand. She had bitten him hard enough to draw blood.

The policeman who seemed to be standing back observing it all suddenly came forward. He pushed the bitten man out of the way and knelt by the bed. He was talking in a sweet way trying to coax her out. The man who'd been bitten stood looking at his hand with a long face. He had a disgusted expression, like someone was pulling his forehead and chin in opposite directions, like his eyes might bulge out of their sockets. All of a sudden he pulled out his gun, knelt down, pointed the gun under the bed, and began shooting. He fired four times.

Something hard and thick filled Max's throat. He couldn't breathe or swallow. The room around him went dark and then came alive brightly, and then went dark, as if someone were turning the lamp on and off. Max couldn't speak. He looked down at his little brother but had a hard time focusing on him.

The police were moving, pushing the two of them out into the front room. One of them noticed that Max's father was still alive, that his arm was reaching up for his sons. The man walked over to Max's father, pointed a gun at his head and pulled the trigger. There seemed to be no thought or feeling involved. Max screamed now with all his strength. He tried to strike the man who shot his father but was pulled back by the policeman who held him. A gun was placed against his temple to quiet him. Max looked over at Abe; he was crying so softly, his little chest heaving in spasms.

"Who should we let live?" The one holding Abe asked.

He pushed Abe, still holding the boy by his neck, closer to Max. Max swallowed, almost vomiting. He felt his body shaking. When he spoke, he was as polite as possible.

"I beg you, he's just a child, barely six. He's a good boy, he deserves to live."

The man loosened his hold on Abe's neck and stepped back as if to let him go.

"This little brother you love very much, don't you?" The man gave him a sympathetic look as he waited for an answer. Max nodded, his eyes full of tears.

The man lifted his arm and pointed the gun at Max. Max closed his eyes, frowned, and bit down on his lower lip. His heart was pounding; it felt like it was echoing throughout his entire body. He could feel its jarring weight in his tight stomach and in his ears and temples.

His entire body flinched as the gun fired.

Max opened his eyes. The man was smiling a wide, sick smile. His arm was sticking straight out from his side, pointing away from Max. Abe's little body shook for a moment as he lay on the floor, and then he was completely still, his mouth slightly open and his eyes searching for something unseen. Max felt his own body go limp. He felt his breath rise up in his throat and catch. His face flushed with cold heat as something in him seemed to break. A choking sound came up from deep inside. The man who'd been holding onto him finally let him slip out of his grip to the floor. Their father's body was off to his right curled up in an unnatural way. Max closed his eyes tightly and curled himself into a ball.

The man who shot Abe was telling the other men to go.

He called to Max, nudging him with his boot, "Hey! You see what happens to Jews? Don't you ever forget." And then that thing, he couldn't be human, turned, stepped over Abe's body, and left.

Present Day

As you've gotten older you've looked back at the grandfather and grandmother that you thought you knew so well. They'd been the kindest people; you saw them with your child eyes, soft, warm, familiar. There were no real mysteries about them. They were the people who loved you most.

With your grown woman mind you tried to understand how the grandmother you always thought you knew came all the way to America when she was only fourteen, by herself, on an old rickety ship. How she sailed in steerage just a week after the Titanic had sunk. How she worked and worked in the sweatshops, sending the money that would eventually bring each person in her family over to be with her, walking miles to work to save money on the streetcar. And you think about how then, once they'd all joined her in Philadelphia, they were struck by The Great Influenza Epidemic of 1918. It makes you cry now when you picture her, the only one of them who didn't get sick, rushing from house to house to care for everyone in the family.

As you age it doesn't get any easier when you think about the grandfather you loved so much. Maybe it gets harder with time. You didn't know that the smallish man with the enormous heart, your grandfather, witnessed the massacre of his entire family during the Pogroms of Kiev. You never knew in your youthful innocence that he was sent to live with an Aunt who abused him. And that he had no one then, only his memories.

What you did know was that your grandparents both came from Kiev, Russia, and that they'd never known one another there. That they met in Philadelphia, and that Max might not have been her first choice, but Emma married him, and he was happy with that. You knew that your grandfather was the kindest grocer in Philadelphia. You knew that they had five children, and that their three sons went to college. And you knew that this family—that you—were what mattered most to them. It was you that gave them happiness.

The Redskin Logo's Soliloquy
for Mark McCaig

The white kiss of toothpaste on the towel's tip
is the same in every bathroom from sea
to shining sea—a mouth is a mouth is a hamster
in a red wheel running its route. But some can run
forever, some say I'm nothing but another How
White Man, but last I checked the notion of tribe died
with the strip mall's lot shimmering like an oil-slick
otter. Maybe my disembodied head has nothing
to barter at the trading post but a moth's thin flutter
beneath a streetlamp, the frantic thwap of wings
fluttering their encore for an audience of slugs.
In D.C. they number schools to teach us
hopelessness. Skin is skin unless it's yours.

Delirium Tremens: Keith Moon at Laguna Beach, 1978

belting at the sunset surf I
can still hit every note in licking

boots for my perks though both
hands quake as if cascading

two crashes in a wave
of cymbal   most Chevys

only run as far as they're built
to run which you can hear

on side two of Surfin' Safari
which is rubbish but

I still blast its syrup
harmonies so loud the draperies

twist   my merman phone
shrieks in its cradle whenever

my craving bells   dear boy
it gabs won't you come get mullered

on Manhattans   dear boy I say
back to the mer-tail

you know California shakes
enough on her own

A Proposition

Steel cock of death, this magnum's barrel
snug against your temple. The round
chambers with the hammer-click
as a blank legal pad lays
beside your bag of bruised
Red Delicious. Of course you're still
in your robe. Sugar Smacks bloat
in a bowl of skim. Your matted hair
looks like a gaggle of wrens
made a nest and fucked until they lost
their appetite for worms. Just play
along. The psycho crook says
sixty seconds is all you get
to ink your own obituary before he blows
the grey confetti of your brains
against the wall. What makes the cut?
Frenching Amanda Gardner
behind grandma's barn one night so ancient
that in the art film of your life
the scene is a winding dolly shot
braced with weepy cellos?
Or do you ravage the stacks
in a library no one haunts—excelsior
grades from an Egyptology elective
your junior year when all you can fit
in the trunk of memory's time machine
is the correct spelling of Tutankhamen?
The house is still as a hay bale.
Your father's hand-me-down clock
ticks its one thin note in the den.
Ok. Maybe after the funeral

you trashed your father's clock,
his nightstand Hustlers and strap-on
candy cane bow tie worn once
a year for the office Xmas party.
I asked you to play along.
Lowest common denominator
of office supplies, the legal pad.
My cop uncle had a pristine stack
on his credenza. His last day on the job
before the short cruise of his retirement
he sat with both feet propped on cheap pine,
the second hand lapping twelve
as he folded plane after yellow plane
to toss at the receptionist, a real
giggle-face, waiting to punch out.

The Myth of Socrates

Apparently, my parents flew to South Korea to adopt me, picking me up stork-like in a sack, to endow me with the comforts they couldn't help but share. They acted out of Irish-Catholic guilt, making a transaction with God, trading me for a ticket to heaven. At least, that's the version of the story I told myself, in order to dismiss the obligations of parental love I was jeopardizing by coming out to them.

There was something about this scene of Saturday morning domestic bliss—Dad paying bills at the head of our oblong dining room table, my blonde-haired, blue-eyed siblings running up and down stairs, opening and closing the fridge, flipping TV stations—that made my words irrelevant, far apart from the events swirling around Mom who, forever patient and kind, turned the pages of the paper and sipped her tea.

I sat down quickly enough to startle them, facing Dad, the long end of the table behind me, rarely filled these days with my three younger brothers and three older sisters. I was ready to burst, having kept this secret for no less than nine years. I'm sure my mouth hung open. Short and paunchy Dad, balding and grey, stopped punching numbers on his calculator. Mom and Dad stared at me, eyebrows raised.

I traced the up-and-down lines of dead wood on the shiny table. Where did my courage go? "I've wanted to tell you for a long time." I felt them become rigid, steel themselves. They paid bills like this every Saturday, whispering to each other. Whenever I walked in, Dad covered his checkbook.

"I think…" I pushed down on my bouncing legs. "No. I know, I'm gay."

Dad leaned back in his chair, revealing the attorney's letterhead, the one who helped me get off with only community service for shoplifting. I knew Dad had worthier financial obligations—my oldest sister's medical school, mortgage payments, soccer uniforms for my younger brothers. I didn't know, after two years, he was still paying off my delinquency.

"That's simply not true," Dad said.

When my best friend, John and I role-played this conversation, I never imagined I'd be affected by their disappointment. How it would stun me. "It's who I am." I glanced at my watch, stood up. "I'm late."

Hidden behind his glasses, Dad didn't seem as tired as he did when he took them off. He bounced the tip of the frames on the table. "We don't condone that lifestyle."

Mom rubbed her hands together, searching our new hardwood floors for answers. She took the back pew to Dad's proselytizing.
"I'm 19. You can't tell me how to live my life."

Dad blocked the doorway. "You're not leaving until we discuss this like men."

Men? I almost laughed. He was out of shape and thirty years older. What made him a man and not me? Because he liked sports? Fucked women? Because he gave birth to daughters every two years and when he couldn't get Mom pregnant, he got scared that he wouldn't have an heir to his throne so he adopted me?

I pushed him out of the way, grabbed my keys. I peeked back, saw Mom helping him stand back up. Mom kept calling my name after I slammed the door. I pushed Dad harder than I wanted to.

There's nothing but sincerity in some things, like windmills. They move quietly, at the wind's disposal. After a night of partying with John, I was hung-over and tired that Sunday afternoon, dozing on and off. The History Channel showed black and white pictures of farmers using windmills as water pumps and grain-grinders. One by one, my brothers, sisters, and Mom sat on the couch next to me, leaving after realizing I wasn't changing the channel to football or cooking shows. I held the remote on my thigh with one hand, and the other rested on Plato's Republic, my favorite book, next to me.

Dad made several trips past me before sitting on the loveseat to my right. He told me about the construction of windmills. He was an architect. When I was a kid, I used to follow him around his office. I wanted to build something together, but now I'm a barback, hoping to become a bartender so I could entice attractive blonde-haired blue-eyed men to bed by giving them free drinks. My parents thought I was a waiter.

Dad's windmill lecture, and avoidance of the obvious topic of my sexuality, made me want to steal again, to make him see I could be worse. But not just steal. I'd parade around the house with the most expensive shoes I could find.

Dad stopped talking, propped his bare feet on the glass table. I wondered if the scrape above his eye was my fault. "Talk to Father Carroll," he said. "Unless you change your behaviors, we can't have you living under our roof. I'm sorry, Garret, but your mom and I have done all we can."

When I was thirteen, Mom caught me in the laundry room with my best friend comparing our pubic hair. She screamed, dropped the laundry basket, and ran. I would've killed to hear how she explained this to Dad: crying, "They were half-naked!" Dad, holding her, "Like Adam and Steve!" Drama queens. As a consequence, Dad made me see Father Carroll for two years.

This time, I didn't respond to Dad's request for the same intervention. Let him think I hated the idea. I let my hand fall off the remote, sunk further in the plush couch, and we sat there, staring at the spinning windmills.

A week later, after teaching his Sunday school class, Father Carroll reached over his desk to shake my hand. "Your dad told me you might show up." One gray spot on his trimmed beard made him appear to blush.

He was an insecure young priest when I last saw him. Since then, stories about his unflappability became legendary—holding the head of a half-decapitated man during last rites, praying over a crack baby while its mother vomited in the baptismal font, looking me right in the eyes when I told him I'm gay. "It's OK," he said.

"The Church doesn't condone my lifestyle."

He held up a hand-written sermon. "God wants us to be compassionate, faithful, loving. Heterosexuality is not a major issue." His beard was new, hid his dimples. Five years ago, he was sweatier, repeatedly clicking his pen.

"Dad disagrees with you."

The office building outside his window seemed greyer than I remembered, possibly abandoned. It wasn't until I had stopped dreading the thought of Father Carroll bringing up the laundry room incident, which never came, that I began to look forward to afternoons playing chess and exaggerating my problems with parents and friends. Then, one sunny afternoon, I had said, "Check mate," and he responded with a wink and a firm squeeze of my bone-thin shoulder. That's when I thought I might be talking to a closet-case.

"I baptized you," he said, meeting my gaze outside the window, drawing me back in. "God loves you. Your family loves you." His bright blue eyes intrigued me. I couldn't help but wonder what secrets we might share.

I walked to the bookcase behind him. Among Bibles and scholarly journals was a shelf of Plato's books. Father Carroll used Plato's Republic to teach me about Socratic dialogue. After our last prescribed session, he let me keep the book.

"Why didn't you teach me about St. Augustine or some Korean saint?" I asked, taking Plato's Phaedo off the shelf.

"I'm due at the hospital so I don't have much time." Father Carroll swiveled in his chair to face me. "Your mind is like mine. It probes and bifurcates. I suspect the Socratic dialogue brought you closer to the truth."

"What we talked about before doesn't help me now. I need an updated dialogue." I rubbed the book's cover with my thumb. "According to the Church, homosexuality is a choice. Therefore, heterosexuality is also a choice."

"This has to be quick." Father Carroll folded his hands on his lap. "Celibacy is a choice, so I agree with you. Sex is a choice."

"Then the gender of the person we're attracted to is also chosen."

"If you choose celibacy, it doesn't matter." He smiled, straightened his starched white collar.

"You're not following the dialogue." I held up the book. "Is it true that we choose whether we're attracted to males or females?"

"I don't believe so. No."

"So same-sex attraction is only sinful if acted upon. Gays must be celibate in order to lead a moral life?" This is what he trained me to do. Brutal honesty. Nothing held back.

He rubbed his palms on his thighs. "According to the Bible, yes. According to me, no. The Church has spent too much time validating the Bible's authenticity, when it should have been helping people distinguish between the undeniable and allegorical."

I picked up his Bible off his desk. "Are the parts about homosexuality undeniable?"

"Jesus's words are the truth. The history of Moses—true. Divine intervention—maybe. Rules dictating what to eat and who to sleep with in Leviticus? Interesting, but not undeniable."

I thumbed through the Bible. "So, the Church is wrong?"

He smoothed out the pages of his sermon on the desk. "I wouldn't say that."

"What would you say? They're ignorant. Judgmental." I held the books together—Plato and Bible—covers facing him. "We can make our dialogue public. You can help me."

"Your position is too one-sided for this to be a true dialogue." He held up his hands. "I'd love to help you, but I have to pick my battles."

"What other battles have you picked?"

He looked at the clock on the wall. "I'm late. Suffice it to say, I'm working on changing the Church's doctrine, but it'll take time. I'm only one man."

I dropped the books on top of his papers, leaned against his desk. "Is the Church's stance on a priest's sexuality undeniable or allegorical?"

He pushed away from his desk. "That's crossing the line."

Halfway through saying it, I knew it was inappropriate, but I couldn't stop the words from coming out. He turned his chair around.

"I'm sorry, I got carried away."

He stood, brushed off his cassock. "I can talk to your dad if you want, but I've said all I'm willing to say."

I held the back of his chair. "My question was hypothetical. It wasn't supposed to have an answer."

He threw his coat over his shoulder. "I'm a practical and pragmatic man. Based on our conversations, hypothetical or not, you should understand that."

The myth of Socrates is that there's a momentum to his dialogue, a core truth to strive for. I reached a dead end with Father Carroll, because I wanted to pursue the issue to its logical conclusion. Wasn't that practical and pragmatic? Wasn't that what he taught me?

I called John, told him to meet me at the mall. He was a philosophy major, but he didn't like talking about "deep stuff" in his spare time. Whatever we did though, he could always make me laugh.

"These were the shoes we were talking about." He flung the shoes at my stomach. He was one of those waify white kids who looked younger than he really was.

I ran my hand along the sole and up its side. Who knew alligator skin would feel so soft, forgiving? Across the shimmering floor, a gaggle of old ladies tried on new faces at the make-up counter.

"Try them on. It'll help us think," he said.

I took off my new sneaker, shoved it under the bench so John couldn't smell my feet. "I can't live at home anymore."

John put his fingers on his lips. "Let me see." He twirled his other wrist.

I spun around. In the shoe mirror, I pretended to walk, my jeans covering the checkered tongue. The shoe couldn't have been more comfortable.

"Those shoes will brighten up your dreary, homophobic home." John looked around for cops, like he used to do before I got caught with a new shoe in an empty box. John hadn't noticed the security guard, and pleaded with the store manager to charge him with the crime.

Taking off the shoe deflated me, as if I was returning from zero gravity. I put it back on its display shelf. "I can't do that anymore."

John rubbed my shoulder. "I'm sorry."

Luckily, the make-up ladies were too preoccupied to notice John's touch. I didn't like drawing public attention since our senior year, when John wiped ketchup off my cheek in the cafeteria. They called us faggots until we graduated.

He slapped my leg. "At least try on both of them to see how good they feel."

I protested, but he grabbed the shoe and walked towards a tiny middle-aged Asian woman sifting through the clothes rack.

"Excuse me." John was a teapot, one hand on his hip and the other cocked to the side. "Pardon me."

The lady looked at him, confused. I could never tell the difference between Koreans, Japanese, Chinese, Vietnamese.

John placed the shoe on top of the lady's overstuffed bag. "Could you get the other shoe? Size 11, please."

"I don't work here," she said.

John's fingers splayed at the collar of his Polo shirt as if he were offended. "That's OK, honey. I won't tell."

She clutched her bag to her chest. "I don't work here." She knocked the shoe on the floor and speed-walked away, looking back to make sure John wasn't following her.

After my initial shock, I couldn't stop laughing. "You don't give a damn, do you? Always messing with people."

"It's interesting." John dusted off the shoe, examined it closely. "People are so afraid to say, 'Fuck off.'" He put the shoe on the shelf. "So are you."

For lunch, I suggested a Korean restaurant where my parents used to take me, trying to force Korean-ness down my throat. John and I lowered our voices to fit the serene surroundings—the small vases with purple flowers on each table, water trickling over a stone fountain, soft-spoken waitresses.

Some words on the menus were misspelled. Instead of "dumplings," they had "dumpings." After we ordered, John asked to keep the menus so we could keep looking for mistakes and laughing.

"All you people no spell good?" John asked, folding his hands and bowing so far that I could see the blonde highlights on top of his head.

I rolled my eyes.

"Funny or mean?" he asked.

We had a rule—mean comments were permissible only if they were funny. "Funny...I guess."

The other customers were Korean. Ate Korean. Talked Korean. My family of nine had to push tables together. We'd recognize the faces of the wait-staff and they'd recognize us, but we never graduated past a cordial nod as they ushered us to a corner.

"I don't feel very feng shui." I opened and closed the sticky menu, the sound like smacking lips.

John's staccato laugh was the only straight-sounding thing about him. "You feel the yin? The yang?"

"Nope," I answered. "No yin. No yang."

John and I had sex the night of our graduation. We joke about it now, since he's mainly attracted to black guys, although he thinks my seventeen-year-old brother is cute, which totally grosses me out. I think we had to have sex in order to reach this level of comfort.

"Why did we come here? You don't even like Korean food," he said.

Our waitress brought soup that tasted like salty water.

"I'm trying to figure out who I am."

"We're some picky queens. That's who we are." John pushed his bowl aside. "Aren't fags supposed to appreciate this exotic shit? Give me a burger and fries any day."

"I thought coming out would make me feel whole. Why do I feel worse?" I stirred the soup with chopsticks. "A Socratic dialogue would help."

"Bullshit. I took that class last semester. Listen to me." John raised his arm, wiggled his fingers at our waitress to bring the check. "You're never coming here again. You're a gay American. You don't need to figure out anything else."

John convinced me to try Ecstasy that night. The dance floor was electric, like an orgy. Whenever someone touched me, anywhere, it was like they were caressing the tip of my penis. I didn't have sex, though, because John told me it would ruin the sensation.

I couldn't fall asleep until the afternoon and woke up at night, the entire family in bed except for Dad, who was working late. I was watching this show about ants when he walked in. I must have looked worse than he felt, because he asked, putting his briefcase on the kitchen counter, "You alright?"

"Just tired." I put my hand on the Republic next to me.

Apparently, one species of ant will kill the queen of a different species, rub the deceased queen's scent all over their bodies, then the stupid victims feed the invaders as if they were the queens. Dad heated up the leftovers and sat on the loveseat. We watched the ants scurry around, desperately searching for food to feed their hungry tormentors.

"I have a cousin who was homosexual," Dad said, tucking a napkin in his starched white collar, his dark blue tie hanging loosely around his neck.

"Which cousin?"

"You never met him. His name was Stuart."

"You said he was gay. Did you change him?"

Dad shook his head. He thought this was mean. John would've thought it was funny. It's all relative.

Dad answered the beeping microwave, ate the lasagna as he walked back. The cut above his eye was almost healed. "Father Carroll called to apologize," he said. "I'm not sure why, but he can't see you anymore."

Father Carroll didn't have the courage to stand up for who he was. It still hurt, though. Either way, it hurt.

"He's a practical and pragmatic man," I said.

"Yeah." Dad chewed and talked at the same time. "He probably is. And a good priest too."

"I'd disagree with any priest."

Dad shoveled two forkfuls in his mouth, cheeks bulging. "I'm sorry, but you know the consequences. We've tried helping you with your drinking and spending problems, but this is the last straw. You can visit, but it's time you suffer the consequences of your decisions."

"I'll pack my bags tonight." I held up Plato. "Want to have one last Socratic dialogue?"

"It doesn't have to be our last, but I'm game." He put his dish on the table.

I tucked my ankle under my leg. "It's the last for me." Before he could ask why, I continued, "If homosexuality is a choice, then all sexuality must be a choice."

"The Bible is clear about homosexuality."

"The Bible also says that women were made from Adam's rib and people, evil people, used that holy book to justify slavery and the Holocaust."

Dad looked at his wiggling toes under the glass table. I could smell his feet from here. "People are sinners, but the Bible is the truth. We're more enlightened today."

I stood, placed my hand on my hip. "Would you disown me if I coveted a neighbor's wife or used the Lord's name in vain?"

"That's different." How could he sit there so calmly? Father Carroll had the same stoic look. That plastic face must be passed on from generation to generation of believers.

"It's not different. A sin is a sin. Fuck God!"

"You're going too far," Dad said, finally sitting up.

"I haven't gone far enough. God sucks, and Father Carroll is a flaming faggot. Did you know that? There it is—the Devil's Trinity—disobeying my father, using the Lord's name in vain, and being gay."

Dad slid his hand slowly down his face, rubbing his five o'clock shadow. "This dialogue is over."

"It's not over until you tell me what you think about me." That's what it came down to. Who am I to him?

He held up his hand. "I wish you wouldn't do this."

He looked sad, but I didn't feel his love. Ants, swayed by chemicals, showed more affection to their adopted torturers.

"Talk to God, because He lost you a son." I folded my hands, bowed until my head touched my knees. If I had a gong, I'd bang the Korean-ness out of me. I won this dialogue. The last thing I heard before I slammed the door was the narrator's voice from the TV, "The invaders are fed as royalty."

I would call John from the car, tell him he has a new roommate. We would go out. Sober, I would fuck the first blonde-haired, blue-eyed man I saw.

An Interview With Vanessa Gebbie

Vanessa Gebbie is the author of two short story collections, Words from a Glass Bubble and Storm Warning, the editor of Short Circuit: A Guide to the Art of the Short Story (all from Salt Publishing), and the forthcoming novel, A Coward's Tale (Bloomsbury). She has previously won the Bridport Prize, the Fish Short Story Prize, and the Willesden Herald Prize among many other honors. She is Welsh and resides in Sussex, England.

You've become fairly well-known for your short stories and now you have a novel coming out soon. Before we discuss your projects and how you write, can you talk a little about your trajectory in becoming a writer? Did you always write or did you come into this game later in life?

The writing bug must have bitten me early, because I wrote a lot as a child and in my teen years. Terrible poetry, mainly. I also started a newspaper, aged six. It only ran to a single issue, had a print run of one, and was written in blue crayon. I then stopped writing until much, much later. Turning 50 started me off again—maybe I had something worth saying after all that time? I started writing short stories seriously in late 2003, had my first publication online in early 2004, my first competition success the same year. 2005-6 saw a mass of stories, small publications, more competitions, setting my sightlines higher all the time. My big turning point was in 2007 with short story successes at "Bridport" and "Fish," and a win at a novel competition run by the *Daily Telegraph*. I haven't really looked back. Writing has been a major part of my life for some years now, whether it is making something new, or teaching, or doing paid critiques for others. I am still learning, and hope I will always do so. I'm off on a Writing for the Theatre course with the Arvon Foundation in August...

Compared to America, Europe doesn't seem to have much of a literary journal culture. Do you see this as an obstacle for European writers of short fiction, or do you think the Internet has closed the gap? Did you find it difficult developing an audience at home? Are there differences in British and American writing in your opinion?

I don't know much about other countries in Europe. The UK has always had lit journals, but perhaps not as many as the USA. New ones are popping up every year here, some allied to the universities where Creative Writing courses are now taught. Some not. In that sense we are behind the USA—our Masters in Writing programs really took off decades behind yours, and the literary journals that seem to start life in order to showcase the writing done by graduates or undergraduates among others, and to give them a go at editing, are correspondingly later in their birth cycle.

Is it an obstacle? Hmm. There is possibly less of a cookie-cutter culture here, a function of our Masters programs hitting the writing world after yours and being able to learn from history—but that may be my own view and not that of others. There has been plenty of recent debate about the effect of university programs on creative writing in the USA, and I don't want to rehash all that—indications are that awareness of the issues may be moving things on anyway, if indeed they needed to be moved on at all. But I have to say—an obstacle to publication in a literary journal is not necessarily an obstacle to original and strong writing, is it? I'll leave that as a question.

The Internet is a marvelous thing, as is any freeing up of the market for writers. However, I do think it has to be treated with caution for many reasons, not the least of which is the potential polarization of writers who do and writers who don't. Some mainstream publishers and literary agents still do not count online publications as meaningful—and I wonder if that is because of the vast numbers of online journals that come and go, the iffy quality of many, and the perception that you can get anything published online of you try hard enough—or indeed, if you start your own journal and publish yourself.

Audiences…all one can do is work hard, get your work out there, accept invitations to do readings, run workshops, accept that funds are tight, do some things for nothing, support others, and that way, slowly, your name begins to get round. If you write what some people like to read, they may tell others. I have a marketing background—and I know that all the marketing in the world won't be as successful as word of mouth.

Are there differences in American writing and British? I am sure there are. The voices will be different. The themes will differ. Some stylistic differences, perhaps—I have a perception that many US literary writers will use long, flowing, weighty sentences, whereas some Brits may not. On the other hand, that may just be the work I choose to read from specific writers, and I'm reinforcing a false belief.

Okay, so I've read quite a bit of your work, first being introduced to you by the One World project, which we were both involved in, and later reading your collections. One of the things I love about your writing is your ability to really give a reader a sense of place. Do you do a lot of traveling and/or research to inform your settings? Do your stories often start with a place versus plot and character?

Thanks Sequoia, that was a terrific project, wasn't it? And thank you for reading my collections, I appreciate that. I love to travel, but don't travel to research my settings. It is hard to analyze one's own work, and often unhelpful for future output, so I'm wary of doing that too much—but I think I am inspired by some alchemy between the essence of a place I know, or what I perceive that place to embody if I don't know it from experience, and character. Whatever the theme of the piece will be (as opposed to the plot/subject) the setting will often inform it as much as the characters.

An example: I know Cornwall in the west of the UK quite well and am drawn to the old tin-mining communities, and indeed the old mines themselves. One mine, now a museum (Geevor and Levant), was the site of a disaster in 1919 when a lift device failed. My character is a young baker returning from the WWI trenches, who can't bake any more—he's seen and done too much to allow him to return to a benign and wholesome job. The dates are right. The conflict embodied in both setting and character is right. Story. See? I won't give it away any more than that!

There is a huge difference between setting as embodiment of theme, and setting as mere window-dressing.

Having written two short story collections (many of the stories in the flash fiction category), did you have trouble making the transition to writing your novel? How did you go about writing *Coward's Tale*? **Do you prefer one form over the other?**

Yes! I had huge trouble. The novel began as a series of long short stories containing the same characters, and in the same setting. Over five years, in between writing all the other stuff, I created 100,000 words. I then needed to undo much of it, to weave it all together so that there was a single clear narrative thread that pulled the reader through, as opposed to a series of related but unlinked stories. I had no idea how to do that with this pile of words, so enlisted the help of a marvelous and clear-headed novelist called Maggie Gee, and thanks to a grant from the UK's Arts Council I worked under her guidance for the best part of another year to revise and polish.

No, I don't prefer one form to another. I think if a piece of work is in the best form for that piece, it sings better than if it was in another shape—I just like work to sing, whatever it is.

In addition to writing, you also teach classes and you've edited a book on the craft of the short story. In the past, you've worked in marketing. If anything, how do these aspects of your life have an effect on your writing? And after having taught for many years and worked with award-winning writers on *Short Circuit*, **what do you think are three of the most valuable lessons journeymen writers should take to heart?**

Well, I love passing on to others this thing I do—opening up their creativity, and "giving permission" is all I see it as. It is easy to list some craft skills, and easy to make up exercises for the practice of those.

More important is the skill that sends a writer to that place within themselves from which flows the strongest work. The work that means something, not just entertainment. The trouble is, that working for long doing that, encouraging others to take risks, necessitates explanation and analysis of a process that doesn't like to be exposed to the light. It dulls my own spark. So I do limit teaching for that reason.

Working with those writers who contributed to *Short Circuit: A Guide to the Art of the Short Story* was a fantastic privilege. I will never forget their passion for what they do, or their generosity in sharing it.

Three lessons for aspiring writers...

1. Walk the tightrope between self-doubt and self-confidence with pride. You need both. Without self-doubt you will never seek to do better. Without self-confidence you will never know when someone else (maybe a much more experienced person) is wrong about your work.
2. Don't be fooled by the loud voices in writing workshops. Listen for the quiet ones. It may be the quietest voice that is speaking the truth.
3. Don't give up. Ever.

(and 4. Try writing when you least want to. When you are dog-tired, or desperately sad, when it seems least likely you will be able to write anything "good." Push through. And don't read it back until the clouds lift.)

Okay, so until now, you've published with Salt, one of the darlings of the independent publishing world. Your novel is coming out with Bloomsbury in both the US and the UK. What are the differences in working with a large publishing house versus an independent? What do you value most in both spheres?

I am very lucky to have had three books with Salt. I am very lucky because firstly, they produce absolutely beautiful books, so the quality of the product is high. Secondly, I am lucky to have had the experience of working as part of a small team with the publisher. Salt is basically a husband and wife team with a young family, dogs, and hamsters. It is not a business with support staff, sales, marketing, etc, etc, although they did have interns to answer the phones, pack up the books and take them to the post and so on. They get the books onto the usual online shops, and sometimes, into the larger real bookstores as well. But you simply have to get involved, spreading the word, remembering to buy your own books to take to many festival venues, for not all have the luxury of a bookshop running the sales. You have to become a sales person, you have to blow your book's trumpet—and why not? It's strange how many writers seem to baulk at doing that—it's all part of it, so get on with it, I say. And, if you can't enjoy, pretend.

Working with the Bloomsbury teams in London and New York has been wonderful, in a different way. I was astonished to find that a whole village would be working on *The Coward's Tale*. When I had completed the final tweaks suggested by my main editor Helen Garnons-Williams, someone else (Audrey) would be copyediting, then the manuscript would be checked and tweaked again by another editor, Erica Jarnes, and I. Someone else again would be proofreading, someone else (Alice Shortland) suggesting brilliant ideas for making a map to give to booksellers, someone else again (Holly MacDonald) designing the cover and the map. It will be Anya's turn next, working on publicity and other marketing initiatives. That's just London. There's Kathy Belden, my New York editor, and Rachel her assistant. Back in the UK there is also a team in charge of regional sales. It is astonishing.

But at no point do I feel I need or want to sit back. At every point, they consult, ask, discuss. I have already set up some readings and events in November and onwards, when the book is out—and other events will come in organized by Bloomsbury. I will go happily to whatever I am pointed at, and enjoy it all.

I value it all. Getting a book out there, however we do it, is what many of us work towards, and I am enormously grateful to Chris and Jen Hamilton-Emery at Salt for giving me my first publishing opportunity, and the repeated opportunities to learn about the process in a very hands-on manner. Bloomsbury, like Salt, is absolutely passionate about the books they publish, and it is just wonderful to be swept up in that. But I know that with *The Coward's Tale* as with all my other books, much of the hard work comes post-publication. And I'm looking forward to it all.

Tell us a little about *The Coward's Tale*. How did you conceive the story? What do you want the reading public to know that will get them to buy your book?

I can do little better than give you the Bloomsbury USA catalogue copy:

> *A poignant first novel about kinship and kindness, guilt and restitution, and the ways in which we carve the present out of an unforgiving past.*
>
> *Nine year old Laddy Merridew, sent to live with his grandmother for reasons he does not understand, stumbles off the bus into a small Welsh town where he begins an unlikely friendship with old Ianto "Passchendaele" Jenkins, the town beggar-storyteller. Through Ianto, Laddy learns of the collapse decades earlier of the coal mine of Kindly Light: a disaster whose legacy has echoed through the generations, shaping lives in unexpected ways. And while Ianto spins the lively stories of so many men and women in this town, it's his own history in Kindly Light that is the story he can't tell.*
>
> *Like Richard Llewellyn's beloved classic* How Green Was My Valley, *Vanessa Gebbie's* The Coward's Tale *richly evokes the tightly bound communities of old Welsh mining towns—their loyalties and betrayals, loves and losses. Like Llewellyn, Gebbie was brought up by Welsh parents, in England. Unlike him, however, she took every opportunity to spend time in Wales throughout her formative years. Her sense of place is evoked with an authentic dark beauty and a heightened, almost magical charm. Her prose is steeped in the cadences that surrounded her as a child. This rich tapestry of a novel is spellbinding and unforgettable.*

I am immensely grateful to the Bloomsbury team for that description. *The Coward's Tale* took five years to write. Maybe more. I wasn't counting. I was however, working for my settings within memories of the place where my parents were born and grew up: Merthyr Tydfil, in south Wales. Memories related to me over the years by my father, who was born in 1915, and was blessed with the sharpest of minds. And my own memories, from a childhood in which time spent with my grandmother and her family was so important. "The setting embodies the themes...." reprise.

While I was still writing the first draft, however, two things happened that tell me *The Coward's Tale* is OK. First, I was told not to write it at all, when I joined a Masters course hoping for help with the structure. I left, fast. I hope my decision to carry on regardless was vindicated by the fact that two years later more than one publisher wanted the final manuscript...

Second, a section sent to a former colleague for feedback was plundered of my carefully crafted creations and the resulting piece was sent out for publication under his own name, behind my back. No one in his right mind would do that unless it was worth the risk.

I think I was being tested. You have to be prepared to fight for something you love. I did just that. I hope readers love it too, and think it was worth fighting for.

What books/authors would you say influence you the most and why?

Thing is, ask me that tomorrow and the reply will be different. I can honestly say that every book I read influences me—either positively or negatively depending whether they are "good" or "bad" whatever those words mean. I read with my writer's hat on, now—learning how to achieve the effects I want to, by seeing how fantastic writers do it. And conversely, learning how to avoid mistakes, making mental notes never to fall into that trap...

Writers/books I would like to mention today are Maggie Gee (great stories told with clarity, lucid prose, meaningful themes—try *The White Family*), Dylan Thomas's *Under Milk Wood* (fabulous imagination, fabulous characterization in so few words, creation of a complete and unforgettable community in so few pages), Jim Crace's *Quarantine* and *Being Dead* (such originality applied to well aired subjects, making them absolutely his own).

And to wrap up, tell me about where all of this writing gets done. Do you have a special place you go to? A space reserved in an attic?

I have to leave home to write. Most of my best work is done at Anam Cara Writers and Artists' Retreat in remote and beautiful West Cork, Ireland.

http://www.anamcararetreat.com/

Women Who Smoke

I was at this bar in Seoul with Neal trying to remember songs. He sat across from me, just like Steve had those first few months here. Outside, the street was gradually darkening. I stared at a blank square of paper on the table and brought the tip of the pen to my lips, hoping that something would to come to me.

The last time I'd been here was six months ago. Steve and I had been sitting in this same booth with the same window that looked out at the same man tending the fire. That was when I told him I knew about the Korean girl. What was her name, I asked him. Steve said, it didn't matter, her name. That it was a mistake. That we never should have moved here together. He never should have invited me. And I said, who do you think you are, the fucking president of the country? I don't need your invitation. I can live wherever the fuck I want. I can go back to Atlanta or move to LA or New Orleans. But guess what, I'd told him, I'm not going to make your life that easy. I'm not going anywhere. And then I poured a full mug of beer from our pitcher and drank it real slow, just to prove it.

Now I took a drink of beer for inspiration. I wrote down "The Logical Song," by Super Tramp. Barry Manilow, "Copacabana." Olivia Newton John, "Have You Never Been Mellow?"

"Where do you come up with those?" Neal lit a cigarette, abandoning his own blank slip of paper. He was British and didn't get the sad beauty of those songs.

"Steve," I said. "He was good with that stuff." I closed my eyes to remember. Then I wrote down a few more songs and creased the paper in half.

"No more Steve. Remember?" Neal blew smoke at the window even though it was closed.

"You asked." I scooted out of the bench and walked across the bar to give the bartender my requests. Behind him, three shelves of albums were stacked like books, old faded things with fraying spines. I tried to make eye contact with the bartender, a cute guy with shaggy hair and a Jimi Hendrix T-shirt, but he acted busy with the computer. I reached over the counter and put the list in front of him. He smoothed it on the counter and nodded.

Back at our table, Neal had refilled my glass.

"You Brits are so well-mannered," I said. I batted my eyes at him and turned up the dial on my Southern accent.

"And all you Southern girls are so charming." He offered me a cigarette, but I shook my head. Too early.

Except for the bartender, the only other people there were two young women at the table behind Neal. Under the bar's dim lights their hair looked like velvet. The girl whose back was to me wore a fitted turtleneck and butterfly clips in her hair while the other had bangs cut straight across and fistfuls of bracelets on her bare arms. In between sips from their bottled beers, the girls chatted rapidly. Their cell phones were displayed on the wooden table, and every few minutes they pounced on the phones to scrutinize new text messages. Between the cell phones was a white pack of cigarettes decorated with pink butterflies. The two girls inhaled the ultra slim cigarettes at the same time and occasionally waved them dramatically in the air when they wanted to emphasize a point. They reminded me of the girl Steve had left me for.

"Such poseurs," I said. "Acting like they're Audrey Hepburn in *Breakfast at Tiffany's*."

Neal didn't bother turning around. "When I first got here I saw a man slap a woman for smoking in the street," he said.

"Why?" I asked, although I thought I knew the answer. Ugly. That's what my mom called women who smoked. Ugly.

Neal tapped his cigarette in the ashtray. "Women weren't supposed to smoke in public."

"Remember what you told me about Zen masters?" I said. "How they would strike people meditating with a stick to help them become enlightened? Maybe that's what he was doing."

Neal smiled his sexy half smile. "Maybe." "Riders in the Storm" was playing. "This place is brilliant," he said. "Why didn't you show it to me before?"

"You mean like in the whole month we've been together?"

Neal shrugged and sang along with Jim Morrison. I looked out the steamed window onto the street. People were coming into the restaurant below, their scarves wrapped around their necks, arms hanging on each other. I felt a pang of hunger and picked a few of the squid-flavored chips out of the basket.

"The other thing that drives me crazy is the bathroom," I said after I'd chewed my squid ring. "They have this little metal ledge above the roll of toilet paper and a wet folded tissue for women to put their cigarettes out in. I mean they encourage it, smoking in the toilet, just to keep the image of the pure Korean girl. What a joke. After a few drinks they're running back to the bathroom to sneak a smoke. Pisses me off because I usually have to go really bad, and these women are taking their time puffing away in the stall. Just so they can pretend to be innocent."

"You'll see an end to it soon enough," Neal said. "You Americans started this whole nonsmoking farce."

"That's just the beginning," I said "In Seattle we have strip clubs where you can't drink."

"And no trans-fat for your chips in New York," Neal said. "Pardon, French fries."

"Fried taters."

"Damn Southerner."

"Fucking Brit." I grabbed his hand and smiled stupidly at him.

The Doors had ended, and Neil Young's "Expecting to Fly" scratched from the LP player. The song was warped and faded—in other words, perfect.

Four Western guys walked in, taking a table near the skinny cigarette girls but away from the windows. They wore baseball caps that hid most of their buzz cuts, pressed shirts and jeans with bright running shoes. US military, enlisted. This bar was about thirty minutes away from the closest base, making it easier to dodge the military's midnight curfew. And here, in a bar like this, they could meet pretty girls.

"Do you know that Alaska has the highest ratio of men to women in the States?" I said. "Women there have their pick." I tucked a strand of hair behind my ears, which were large for my face and stuck out. I kept my hair long to hide my them, but sometimes I forgot or didn't care, and I'd expose my elephant ears to the world. "They sell T-shirts in Anchorage that say 'Baby when you leave here you'll be ugly again.'" I paused, waiting until Neal smirked to show he got the joke. "If it weren't so damn cold there I'd go to Alaska someday, just to see what it feels like to be those military guys at that table," I said.

"Who cares about them anyway?" Neal closed his eyes. He was handsome in that slightly pale, British thespian way. "They're just generating negative energy, and if you think about them you'll do the same."

"Sounds like more of that Buddhist stuff," I said.

Neal opened his eyes and straightened his back so that he suddenly seemed much taller. "As a matter of fact yes. It's really helping me."

"How's that?" I leaned toward him, hoping that he would meet me across the table and kiss me.

"Well, I'm learning to detach from daily annoyances," he said. "I'm learning that violence does not solve problems. I'm learning that your irrational, emotional outbursts have nothing to do with me." He pronounced the words clearly and distinctly, like he was reading a diagnosis from a textbook.

I traced the edge of the ashtray with my index finger. Still too early in the evening to throw it at him. "Well excuse me for feeling," I said. I slid out of the bench and stomped to the bathroom. On the way, I stopped by the bar and scribbled a hasty request and slipped in a folded five-thousand won note with it to make sure it was played.

The women's bathroom opened to a bare sink and a single stall door, which was locked. A thin wisp of smoke trailed up to the ceiling above the stall. The toilet flushed and the turtleneck girl emerged. She was wearing tight, black pencil pants and spiky heels. She ignored me as she left the room, not even washing her hands. In the stall, a lipstick-ringed cigarette butt in the metal tray glowed its dying embers.

Next to the toilet, the trashcan was empty except for a few wadded tissues. By the end of the night it would be overflowing. Toilet paper clogged the ancient city pipes, so it was forbidden to flush it. While I peed, I perused the graffiti and found my contribution: "Jasmine & Steve TLA" scrawled in the middle of a big heart. I took out the pen in my pocket and tried to scribble over Steve's name, but the tip wouldn't write on the concrete wall. So I spat on it.

When I emerged from the bathroom, the turtleneck girl and her friend had transported their cell phones, cigarettes, and bottle beers to the table with the military guys. I sat back down and refused to look at Neal, who was singing, "And so Sally can wait, she knows it's too late

as we're walking by, her soul slides away, but don't look back in anger."
Oasis. His request, no doubt.

Outside the city was too bright for stars. On the street below people were walking arm-in-arm, bundled in groups of threes and fours, steaming the air with their laughter. A man on the side of the street was busy bringing the large hot coals from the fire he'd been tending into the bulgogi restaurant. Finally I faced Neal.

See that girl with the bangs and the bracelets?" I asked.

Neal twisted his head.

"Don't be too obvious. They were sitting behind us, but they're with those military guys now."

"And?"

"I think that's the girl Steve left me for," I said.

"So?"

"Well, it pisses me off."

"Maybe it's not her," he said.

"It is." But I wasn't sure. I had only seen Steve with the girl once when I'd stumbled upon them one night in another bar down the street from this one. I'd seen bangs, though, and bracelets, before I ran out.

I drained my beer, thinking that there never seemed to be enough in my glass. My request came on then, the one I'd slipped the bill for "Both Sides Now." I sang, "It's love's illusions I recall, I really don't know love at all." Neal just shook his head, wrote something on a piece of paper and went up to the bar. He sat back down across from me, his eyes narrowed. When his song came on, he gave a satisfied smile.

"American Woman, stay away from me, American Woman, mama let me be," he bellowed out of key. I laughed and joined in, singing even louder than him. When the song was over, I moved to Neal's side of the table and kissed his neck. He filled my glass, leaving an inch of foam at the top. I felt his knee rub mine, and I wanted to go back to his place and have sex right then.

The bar was getting more crowded. A few tables of Koreans, college-age, thin with glasses were air-guitaring to Bon Jovi. The girls with them were dressed up in heels and held tiny purses in the crook of their arms. They looked like they'd much rather be somewhere not so dark and dingy, a place that served colored cocktails. They were biding their time.

All the tables were full now, which meant the time for me and my song requests was over. We were having territory problems. Cigarettes were borrowed. Neal's lighter was appropriated. Beers were poured, empty glasses abandoned on our table. More and more people were hovering over our table. Prime real estate.

"Love Shack" was on and the small clearing that passed for the dance floor was packed with revelers grinding under the newly installed strobe lights. The two girls had disappeared, and the Westerner's table had been taken over by a group of Korean salary men, their ties loosened, their drinking furious. Four Korean girls sat where the original two had, behind Neal. I danced near them so I could watch them. They were scheming. After the song was over, I scooted in next to Neal and waited.

One of the military guys I recognized from earlier, dark skinned, Hispanic probably, shoulders twice the width of Neal's, sat himself and his beer down across from us and ground his cigarette out in our ashtray.

"Excuse me, this seat is taken," Neal said.

"I don't see anyone here," the guy said.

"This is our table. Someone is sitting here."

"Who?" The man turned around dramatically and surveyed the bar. While he wasn't looking, Neal flicked the ash of his cigarette into the guy's beer. "I don't see anyone sitting in this chair except me," the man said.

"He's in the loo." Neal blew smoke in the guy's direction.

"You're a very rude guy." The military man shook his head and took a long swig of his beer. He smiled at me, all fake polite. "What about you? Do you mind if I sit here?" The man's ears looked like they belonged to an elf.

"Why are you here?" I asked. "It's twelve-thirty. Past military curfew."

He looked around, shrugged.

"What's your name?" I asked.

"I'm Ron from New Mexico. There's nothing there."

"Ron from New Mexico, how can you justify those wars?" I leaned forward and touched the gold cross he wore on a chain around his neck. "How, Ron, how?"

Ron's smile disappeared. He looked at the table. "I'm not a bad guy," he said. Then he stood and left.

"Well done," Neal said, giving my thigh a squeeze.

It wasn't over, though. I watched Ron watching me from the other end of the bar. He towered over the Koreans. He lit his cigarette with a Zippo, then began chatting with some nearby girls.

Neal's back was to me as he was busy lighting the slim delicate cigarettes of the girls behind us. He spoke to them in semi-fluent Korean. The bar had long stopped playing our songs. I had to go to the bathroom again. I held on to the table for support as I stood. Neal didn't even see me go.

The bathroom door was locked. I sighed and leaned against the wall. The door in the men's bathroom was open slightly, and no one was waiting so I walked in. Ron from New Mexico was zipping his pants at the urinal.

I backed away slowly into the hall. When he came out he brushed my shoulder. "Can I have a cigarette?" I asked.

Wordlessly he tapped out one of his Marlboro Reds and placed it between my lips. Then he lit it with his Zippo. The girl's bathroom door was open now. Once inside, I locked the stall door and peed, tossed my used toilet paper into the now overflowing trashcan. After I flushed, I stayed in the stall and smoked next to the tiny window that looked out into the alley. The ashtray was stuffed with half-smoked cigarettes, so I flushed my butt down the toilet. When I came out Ron was still there.

I fell into him. He smelled like one of the boys in my high school I dated a long time ago. "So," I whispered into his ear. "How dangerous is North Korea? Really?"

He had his hand on the back of my neck so that his lips grazed my earlobe. "I don't know. I just do what they tell me. I'm not a bad guy. Really."

"Me neither. Not really," I said.

We were kissing then, the Marlboro Red fresh on my tongue and the scruff of his military haircut rough on my cheek.

Then there was a hand on my shoulder pulling us apart. Neal's eyes looked red and tired. His free hand gripped his half-full mug of beer. He dropped his hand from my shoulder, shook his head, and turned away. Then, he spun around and tossed his beer on Ron's chest. I grabbed for Neal, but my hands came up with air.

Before I ran out the bar, I bummed another Marlboro Red from Ron. After he lit it, he told me to disappear. It was that time of night. Halfway down the stairs, I slipped and tumbled to the bottom. People on the street, drunk themselves, stepped over me, delicately. The fire man walked past, carrying hot coals in his tongs for the groups of people in the restaurant. I stood up, shaking, and brought the cigarette, miraculously still lit and in my hand, to my lips.

Neal appeared from around the corner then, his body coiled tight. He walked straight up to me and slapped me, knocking my cigarette out of my mouth into a puddle on the street. And even though I knew Neal was gone for good, I called his name as he disappeared into the drunken crowds, then Ron's name, then Steve's, then all the names I could remember, one after the other, words from a song I still didn't know.

Rick Marlatt

How To Forget The Words To Sweet Caroline

There were two down
in the twelfth

when the rain cleansed
its silvery hands

over the first pitch's memory,
its dark beers, and sunset.

While the few hundred
left scattered

for the warmth of hands,
roofs, garbage sacks,

we stood on our seats,
we let water come at us.

I cupped my palm around your neck,
pressed my lips into yours,

your hair trailed the cool yellow
of weeping river lily.

We prayed for the longest
night in history,

hoping September would
wash us away.

The stereo blasted words
we could've lived by

but you wanted to dance
on the dugout instead.

I'll always love you
just for that.

How To Stay Young Forever

I like to bartend wedding receptions
mostly to serve elderly strangers,
where I can pour an old woman
a glass of red wine, slide it across,
watch her fingers quiver for a grip.
When she raises the glass to her lips,
her tremble holds the world on fire.
A small splat maroons the bar top,
with innocent surprise she looks up,
grey eyes humming Patsy Montana.
Next to her the old man ceremonially
removes his russet handkerchief
from a suit he wore before the sleeves
were frayed, before the auburn soured,
before he realized he'll be buried in it.
He mops a loving circle, a quiet dervish,
light shimmering off his glasses,
her thin hand covering his, guarding
yet another Saturday night secret.
Together, they wipe the spill, untwisted
bones singing inside lavender skin.

Gordita's Ride

The woman trips when she gets off the bus. I watch her pick herself up, never taking her eyes off her book, never looking back at the 470 line and the Mexican boys in the back seat who are whistling loudly about her fat ass. Her face contorts, rises and falls with every sentence of the hot pink, paperback novel with gold metallic letters raised like Braille on the cover. Her frumpy face twitches with wet kisses, heaving chests and cupped breast on the page. The back of her hand reaches up to wipe her nose leaving a track of snail like slime across her cheek, like a trace of sixth grade Bonnie Bell lip gloss. She's oblivious, engrossed. I want to be like that, concentrating like that, but my own spying makes me wonder if anyone ever watches.

I take two hours to dress each morning, trying on whatever makes me look twenty pounds lighter on the earth, easier on my feet. How much space am I taking up, and how much is she? Today, I am having a mass transit breakdown—full of the injury of my own contempt. I wanted to call that woman a fat ass in Spanish too. Just like the boys in the back of the bus must know, I'm a fat lady too.

I'll be meeting the man who buys me drinks. He's never once offered me a ride. He likes my stories of downtown Los Angeles to the Orange County border so much that he never offers me a ride, even when we were going in the same direction. It is stupid of me to hang on to a man who won't even give me a ride home. It's part of my act he says. I stun him with tales of the not so modern world: of pee-stained bus benches and carbon monoxide dizzy spells. We lower-class bus riders with our naked heads exposed from lack of bus stop shelters amuse him. When I met him, I thought I was in for a little middle class charity, my prince come to rescue me off the line. He drove a classic car, his degree and his government job around my poverty. Me? He didn't seem to be bothered by the fat, I could tell great bus stories and I could do—other things.

Every time he met me for a drink, he wanted a story. On good 470 line days when I waited only two minutes for the bus that sped down the freeway and Beverly Boulevard in less than two hours, I would have nothing to tell him. There were days when I sat staring out the graffiti scratched window and watched the perfect orange and purple sunset fill the horizon as we crossed the concrete bed of the San Gabriel River. There were days when nobody tried to pick me up or put me down: the days of invisible fatness, my favorite days. I eased slowly into the window side of a bus seat until I wasn't there at all. On those days, I'd have to fake my adventures with an old story he hadn't heard yet. Sometimes I just told five minutes of the ride and saved the rest for a dry spell. How was he to know if my stories were an hour ago or a year ago? Would he believe a half-naked man peed all over the front seats? That a man with rancid smelling pus oozing out the side of his head coughed up green phlegm on the side of the window and a fly got stuck in it? That roaches crawled into the diaper of a baby whose mother watched, but didn't panic? That all these things happened in a single hour of time?

I describe for him the shrinking little man who wore baseball caps of various construction companies and Pepsi Cola T-shirts. I watch as his eyes sneer. The shrinking man's wife is a hooked-nose crone with yellow-white hair pressed to her sagging breasts. She wears a Camel cigarette paper jacket and a tank top three sizes too small. A roll of flesh pokes out between her tank and threadbare, snap-buttoned corduroys. I wanted to pluck out the hairs in each mole of that roll that stared down the aisle at me.

"They get on every afternoon in Montebello," I tell him. They hold hands so tightly you can smell their sweat mixing.

"Are they retarded?" he asks eagerly.

"I think they're all right," I say, though I'm not sure what all right is anymore after riding the bus so much. We seem to all be on a number line of all right to not so all right; they are closer to not all right.

When we get to Whittier, they are screaming about each other's infidelity and the coming of our Lord Jesus Christ. I stare at them and try to picture Jesus wanting to see them or some nefarious Romeo wanting her, him. I pray "four more stops, just four more stops" in my head like a mantra. Four more stops to my own infidel and savior. The old crone wife has lost her patience. She spits at him and announces to the whole bus, "I'm divorcing this loser pig."

The loser pig is chewing something; I'm thankful I can't quite make out what it is from my seat. The loser pig gets up in her face. I lean forward. I can see the drool on his lips as he bellows so loud the students near the back with their headphones on look up.

"I haven't loved you for years," he screams. He jumps up and pulls down on the "Stop Request" rope without taking his eyes off of her eyes. Both sets of eyes are caked with the yellow crusts of sleep and the oil from dirty fingers rubbing on their lids. They push each other as they get off the bus. They get off at the mobile home park by Lucky's supermarket. From the window, I watch him reach for her left hand.

"Damn, Elena" he says, "that's pretty good. That's worth at least two drinks, if not three." I beam a smile back at him and tell the bartender to bring me a Stoli on ice with a twist of lemon. He never buys me a drink without at least one gritty detail.

If this is the attention he will give me, I take it. He doesn't know this, but I observe him too. I like the smooth chubby bottom of his ear and the palm of his hands as they fold around my shoulders when he greets me. Before I see him, I practice my dialog in my compact mirror mouthing every description of the ride. I am his actress, and I will talk my way through drinks and never dinner so that I do not eat in front of him. He will watch every syllable be chewed and smile at me. I will live on words, his smiles, and air.

He wants to fuck humanity, visit each weird human idiosyncrasy with his cock. He's an artist on the weekends—but he's scared. Doesn't want to be so close he can touch humanity, so he just touches me. His world is getting thinner and thinner, niner to fiver, no time for art projects and afternoons at the racetrack. I'm a healthy looking woman. I look like I was raised on a farm, my grandfather would say. I can feel my grandfather grinning at me when I'm walking down streets or sucking in my gut on the bus. He laughs, "Gordita! Gordita! Always, my Gordita."

I know the disapproval behind the greeting, my grandfather or my drink-buying lover. I am harmless, I am to be ignored. He will not give me rides; he has demons in his eyes. They chant "no other man will fuck you, but me." With the waistline of a redwood tree, I crash to the forest floor with a large sound of ecstasy. I don't love him; I wait for him to let me go.

A boy with socks that meet his shorts at his knees sits with his dad on the seats across from me. He's maybe seven. The tattoos on his

Dad's arms are unreadable through his wrinkled, leather skin. They live in Puente Hills, I hear, or at least the boy does. Junior tells his dad he likes how the other men respected him when "it" went down today. Dad turns white with panic..

"Junior, don't tell your mama where we went."

"I'll just say we visited some of your friends."

"Nah, I don't have no friends she wants you around."

"I ain't telling her nothing. I'll just say," the boy motions widely and rolls his eyes, "I went with you to do some business."

"Naw, son, don't tell her shit. Just say we went to the zoo or something."

"There's a zoo? Can we go sometime?" the boy asks.

"Tell her we spent the day at the mall," says his father who spits out the window when we turn the corner and pushes the brim of his hat low over his eyes.

I am in love with his attention and his lies. When both cease to flow freely from his ears, his eyes and his cock, I may lose interest, too. Fat girls can lose interest too. It's kind of a secret, but it's true. I'll just dream of the boys in the back seat of the bus. I'll think of how we could spend their parole time.

"Owww! Look at her. Hey that was my friend on the inside! Hey, Kathleen! When you get out?" The woman half way up on the driver's side is shaking, jumping up and down. Getting on the bus is, Kathleen. Kathleen, a skinny wrinkled white woman who looks as if you stretched between all the wrinkles with a heavy cleaner you still couldn't scrub her face clean, looks up at the woman. Kathleen is sporting torn lavender sweats and huarache sandals that are as loose as flip-flops, and it's cold outside.

"I got out three days before Christmas," Kathleen says.

"Is that your husband?" The woman on the bus, dressed in denim and rhinestones and bubble-blue plastic shoes points to a wobbling man leaning against the rail on the side of the fare box. He searches his pockets for nickels and dimes. He's counting out "ten, fifteen, twenty cent." It's a long way to $1.35—and there are two of them to buy bus fare for.

"Yup," Kathleen's yellow eyes sparkle, "that's him." She stands, fixing her back taller; I can hear it crack and grow. We all watch as the driver nods his head "sorry" and asks Kathleen and her man to get off and tells them that the bus costs $1.35 and he can't let them ride no more for free. Kathleen slumps over again and backs off of the bus without turning around.

"Good to see you," the woman on the bus waves and moves from one side of the bus to the window where she can see Kathleen sitting on the urine- and gum-stained curb. She turns around and stares us all down.

"Shit," she yells disgusted, "all this time we talking about our men, she made me think like she had something. Talking on the inside 'bout how wonderful he is. I thought he must be a doctor or something."

Shit, I thought about what I had. Broke me, flat-tired down.

It took too many days taking five hours to get anywhere. I needed to feel like I belonged to the southern California air—the brown haze wine that only native Angelenos can drink unaffected. I bought a used car, and then he dumped me. I cried. I clutched my stomach and kept trying to push it in. Down the streets I walked, car keys in hand. Spies are hard to come by, I thought. He'll be back.

Couldn't I observe people from the sidewalk or from my car window? Couldn't I spy on the world around me from the security of the car with no one to notice that my flesh hangs over the side of the seat and encroaches on the emergency brake? Couldn't I have relayed the secret passions of parking lot attendants and nose pickers on the 605 freeway instead?

"You've lost your edge," he had said when I showed up with a kiss for his cheek and no words for his ears. I tried to tell him that I was in every vignette I ever told him, that I had more to say, but I had ceased to be interesting. He paid for his own drink and hesitated for a moment about whether to pay for mine. I missed his warm mouth. I already missed how he held my hand in public on the barstool. I put down my own ten dollars and grabbed my keys.

I sing along to the radio in my car. I listen in amusement to all the advertisements. There are whole cities I drive by on concrete and steel that I saw once in a dream on a bus. I change routes on a whim, new ones and scenic ones. My life is an hour from anywhere and I do not stop for lunch. Without him, I am growing thin.

On Getting Older

Let's face it: I'm getting older. I'm not quite old yet, but I'm not exactly young either. I remember the great The Who lyric: "I hope I die before I get old." Well, so did I, but it didn't happen. And now I'm getting old and so is The Who.

Things ache. Joints get mysteriously stiff. Hands and fingers and feet swell. Teeth like dead bullets in my mouth, waiting to shoot free. Eyesight blurry. Inflamed spleen. Rumbling intestines. Horrible indigestion. Acid heartburn. Sinus headaches. Mouth ulcers. We don't need to go on with this, do we?

I've put on weight. It's the Cokes, one right after another, while I write. I love writing, but it's killing me. I smoke too much when I write. I don't exercise. There are knots in my back. My fingers throb. I have to stand up and walk around the room in the middle of thoughts and sentences. Big bad Jim Valvis. It hurts when I pee.

To counter this, I've begun taking walks around the apartment complex. While I was on the plane going to San Diego, I listened to some guy on the radio who said if you walk ten thousand steps a day you will see tremendous improvements in your health. He said most people get that in their normal daily activity. I figure I get about five hundred.

So I've begun walking around the apartment complex. I walk down to the mailbox, then through the pathway into the center of the complex, and then into the tennis courts. Once there, I walk around and around the courts until I get to two thousand steps. That brings me up to 2,500. Still not enough, but it's something.

What do I think while I walk? I think I hate all of you. I think about how much I'm unappreciated by you all and that when I have a heart attack on this tennis court you'll all going to miss me and be sorry. Then I think about *The New Yorker* and I realize they'll probably take a story after I'm dead, just to spite me. It'll come in the mail the very day after I die. Yes, Jim, thanks—we'll take "My Big Fat Butt Fried in Butter" for our next issue of *Story* magazine.

Well, it's too late. I'm dead. I'm so dead even dead doesn't describe how dead I am. And not only am I dead, but now I'm bitter, too. All those years in the trailer, toughing it out, living on raw roaches and iron deposits. I waited all those years to make it and now I have made it and what happens? Death. My butt in a piano box. That's not right. I'm going to be the kind of ghost who spits green.

Well, these are the things I think about while I walk around and around the tennis court. Then I start to get paranoid. I suddenly know I am being watched. There are condos all along the tennis court and every one of those condos have windows—like little sniper hideouts. Yeah, they're up there watching Fatman Fattenheimer walk around that tennis court, trying to hold off death one more day, so I can get my due. Probably cheering on my death too—waiting for me to drop. It's like a television show to those peep freaks. Look at the fat man go. Wow, that guy's old. Hope I never get that old.

Then it starts raining. It's always raining around here. Then I'm not only old, I'm wet. I'm only on step seven hundred or so—I don't know, I lost count—so now I've got another 1300 in the rain. And I start thinking what a moron that guy was on the plane's radio. I mean, really. If that guy was anybody important, if he was anybody who knew the least little thing about anything, he surely wouldn't be on radio. He'd be on television, or he'd have a hotdog cart.

I used to know a guy who had a hotdog cart in Jersey. He was from Turkey, and he spoke in a booming voice like somebody who was dead needed to hear him. I'd tell him everything about everything. I'd stand by his cart and tell him how much I hated my parents and school and my friends and girls and football and Sunday school and whatever else came to mind. It was sort of like a bartender for an eight-year-old. I let it all out. "You eat hotdog," he'd say to me. "Make you feel better."

"I don't need no hotdog," I said.

I was a tough little bastard.

Then I ate it anyway.

I have a hard time staying awake anymore. I'm up one minute and then I'm in the bedroom the next. I can't face this fact. I tell my wife I'm going to read. "Goodnight," she says.

I no longer go to beaches or pools. I'm ashamed of my gut. That's one sign you're getting older. You start feeling like sunbathing is as stupid a thing as a person can do. You start talking about melanoma, too, as if a Greek man has any chance of catching a disease caused by the sun. Hell, the only Greek who ever got killed by the sun was Icarus, and he had to go shake hands with it to get his ass burnt. But me, I can't go into the sun. Melanoma.

I stay away from concerts and parties too. But I always stayed away from them. I can't be sure if aging has anything to do with that. But I notice that now "get-togethers" really bother me. I haven't time for such petty stuff. I've got to write, and I've got to clip my toenails. And what the hell is going on with them, anyway? They're not the toenails I remember. Somebody took my toenails and replaced them with these mangled, gnarled, blackened things. I went to clip them the other night and the clipper wouldn't go through them. They were too brittle, too gnarled. Anyway, I'm busy trying to beat the clock, and I don't have time to go see what's her face and who's that guy. Time is running out. I've got to get my due.

I wrote in a story a long time ago that it wasn't proper for a man to get old. I was right. A human being is not meant to make it to thirty. He's supposed to get just old enough to reproduce, and then he's supposed to get out of the way. Well, screw that. I'm a modern man. I've got things due me that only age ninety will produce. That's a lot more years. How many steps is that, Mister Plane Radio Genius?

The other day I was finishing my walk when I saw a young girl skipping into the tennis courts. She couldn't have been any older than ten. I flexed up. Big bad Jim Valvis. Yeah, I still had it. Toughest mother on the block. Always have been, always will be. The girl looked at me and smiled. She asked me what I was doing. "I'm getting older," I said.

"You look it," she said.

I would have hit her if I thought I could take her.

Precession

The day that winter came quickly to Scarborough, Lindsey Fitz was institutionalized. Robby Fitz, the preacher, enrolled her in the facility before hanging himself. Robby was a man with darkness inside of his heart, but that was a secret that went to his grave. He died with a sermon plan in his pocket.

This was when the fall left Scarborough. On Monday, flies buzzed around local lemonade stands. The trees were full and green. On Tuesday, the flies were suspended in frozen juice. The leaves suffocated in snow. The lake froze without a minute's notice, taking thirty people on a permanent swim.

On this day, Kasey Woodgrove stood outside of the Bitterbrush Institute, barefoot in the grass. Kasey and Lindsey Fitz had made cookies with their fingers covered in the same dough. When the snow stuck his toes together, he didn't notice.

"Any act of love is an act of faith. Kasey, get those string beans off the burner."

"Yes'm."

"The reason why the reverend locked her up is because he didn't want to see his daughter in league with the devil. It broke his heart."

"Aunt Marian, do you have to talk about this right now?" Riley Woodgrove asked.

Aunt Marian, who was rocking too close to the fire, propped the knitting needles and skeins of yarn against her chair.

"It said in the paper that she tried to escape last night. She should be jailed. She's harm to society."

"How's she a harm to society?" Kasey asked from the kitchen.

He was blending smoked string beans, two ripe mangoes, and fresh salmon in the blender.

"She took the fall away seven years ago, that's how. And the thirty lives that went with it. Not to mention my roses."

"Lindsey Fitz didn't have anything to do with your roses," Riley said. "She was just a crazy. Her and her father were both crazies."

"Something happened to Lindsey Fitz the day that fall disappeared." Aunt Marian knit ferociously. "She was detached. You could see it in her eyes. She got separated from her soul."

"If anyone is detached around here it's Kasey," Riley observed. "What's that noise?"

"Smoothie."

"Sounds like you're blending an animal."

Kasey Woodgrove poured the concoction out of his blender and into a thermos. He placed it in front of Riley.

"Mind if I have a sip?" Riley asked.

"Sure."

"It's kind of gooey."

"It's the salmon."

"Salmon. That's really something." Riley set the blended beverage on the coffee table.

"The salmon was something, before it got killed and then torn apart in the blender."

"You're twisted," Aunt Marian said.

Kasey watched the sun cascade through the vertical blinds. "Snow's tomorrow."

"Aren't you going to salt the roads, boy?"

"Yes. I'm gonna salt the roads."

"Well get to it then."

Kasey got to it.

"That kid." Aunt Marian shook her head.

"I've noted a huge improvement in his behavior," Riley said.

"The stupid doesn't stick out as much as it used to. He still wets the bed sometimes. And he rubs his hands together when he gets nervous."

"He made an entire model of Scarborough in toothpicks."

Salting the roads was Kasey's yearly ritual. He was ready. He snapped his helmet, purple with yellow flowers, under his chin. He slung the salt over his shoulder and hopped on his scooter.

"Oh look," Mrs. Fathurst said, looking out her window. "It must be time to save my daisies."

A local bum changed his cardboard sign from I AM BLIND, GOD BLESS U to I AM BLIND FREEZING GOD BLESS U.

Mr. Woodfence, the owner of the general store, put his suntan lotion on sale.

The snow fell leisurely over Scarborough.

No one died except for a puppy and five hundred lake fish that no one knew about.

"This Christmas, like any Christmas, is a celebration. But this Christmas is a time to help those less fortunate than us. We have to share God's love with them, lest they burn in the fires of hell, where there is weeping and gnashing of teeth. Have a merry Christmas. There are flyers in the foyer if you are interested in sharing God's love with your friends and family."

"Did you hear that?" Aunt Marian whispered to Riley. "Flyers in the foyer."

"Flyers," Kasey said. He got the flyers for Aunt Marian, who was leafing through her hymnal with her right hand. In her left hand, there was a book of matches.

"Fires," Kasey murmured.

"What?" Her eyes were sharp like a cat's.

"Here are the flyers."

"Thank you Kasey. Help me get to my feet."

"Where we going?"

"We're going to the Bitterbrush Institute. I want a look at this Fitz girl."

The Bitterbrush Institute was still white and eight stories high. Kasey's toes stuck together in the snow.

Upon request, Kasey pushed the elevator button. His heart flew inside his ribs like a bat.

Room 833.

She lay in a pile of white blankets.

"Lindsey, some visitors." The nurse smiled.

"Hi honey, we came to check in on you," Aunt Marian said. "It's been a while since you've seen us. You recollect my nephew?"

"I don't."

"Well, you might remember something about us. Kasey's uncle, he died in the lake."

"I don't."

"Well, I hope you're having a fine Christmas," Aunt Marian said. "I hope the food is to your liking. Do you like the snow?"

Lindsey Fitz just lay.

"You like the snow. Thomas, that was my husband's name, didn't like the snow. He liked the summer. He liked fishing on the lake. Do you like the lake?"

"I like lakes."

"Tell me girl. Have you ever accepted Christ?"

"Once."

"Do you fear the devil?"

"No."

Aunt Marian brought the matches out of her pocket.

"Are you afraid of hell?"

"Aunt Marian." Kasey pressed her shoulder.

Aunt Marian struck a match.

"Are you afraid of fire like this burning you all over your body?"

"Aunt Marian!"

"Ma'am. That's enough. If you and your nephew don't get out of here, I'm going to call security." The nurse ushered them out of the room and into the elevator.

"Riley, are you awake?" Kasey stared at his glow in the dark ceiling stars.

"I'm up. What is it?"

"Did Aunt Marian ever try to burn me up?"

Riley, who was sorting the bills, suspended his work. "What are you talking about?"

"Did Aunt Marian light me on fire when I was a little kid?"

"Not to my knowledge." He laughed.

"She has an obsession with fire."

"She just doesn't like the cold. Since Uncle Thom died, she hasn't liked the cold."

"Since he froze in the lake."

"Shouldn't you be sleeping?"

Kasey studied the stars. He plied them with questions. Against their reflection he saw Lindsey Fitz's face. His feet had stuck together.

"I have come to see my very endeared friend, a certain Lindsey Fitz."

"Listen, I can't let you in here unless you're a blood relative."

"I made her a smoothie."

"Well. Alright. But make sure you leave that scooter outside."

"Should I take off my helmet?"

Lindsey smiled a wobbly smile. "Who are you?"

"I made you a smoothie. It contains strawberries, some pineapple ice, and melted syrup."

"Sit down," she said.

He sat down. Lindsey Fitz smelled like nutmeg and dry grass. She drank her smoothie.

"They say you took the fall away," Kasey said. "Why do they say that?"

"When people forgot the beauty of sadness, the fall became a seed and hid inside my heart."

"Can't you get it removed?"

"It's not in the heart that you can see."

Kasey held the girl of rustling leaves and pulled the sheets over, so that neither of them could see.

While Kasey Woodgrove and Lindsey Fitz fell asleep under the white sheets, Aunt Marian purchased a bottle of kerosene.

Riley lit a cigarette at the park. He watched a child skate circles on the lake.

"Hey kid," Riley said. "It's not safe to skate on this lake." He blinked without comprehension.

Riley sat at the banks of the lake, and he thought. The smoke curled out of his lips, and he thought about how people who had beating hearts were as dead as the fish that had frozen with the lake.

The ice split in every direction. Fish burst out from the cracks, wheezing for breath. Instantaneously, the lake flowed free, and the boy fell to the floor, because his skates were so heavy. But he didn't sink. The water was shallow.

"Hey," he said. "The institution's on fire."

Riley put his cigarette out.

"Fire," Kasey said.

"Throw me out the window," Lindsey said.

The air was freezing, smelled like fresh ice and cold cement, and dizzied the hospital drapes. Kasey held Lindsey's hands from behind. He felt the width of her arms and the pressure of her breathing as a pattern with his breathing. He opened the drapes and cradled her against the window sill.

He threw her out the window.

Sunshine spilled out of her pockets. Red, orange and yellow leaves fell out the linen wings. Snow disappeared. Flowers curled underground. The trees lit up with vermillion light, destroying the ice and the salt beneath the ice. The lake liquefied.

Kasey watched from the eighth floor as Lindsey's white dress danced in the autumn wind.

Fists

Go as far as you dare in the heart of a lonely land, you cannot go so far that life and death are not before you.
Mary Austin, "The Land of Little Rain"

In the stern of a Grumman canoe, it is easy to swell with an illusion of your own invincibility and control. Flipping the Grumman requires a dedicated spirit, or else extreme flippancy with canoe etiquette. It is less a canoe than a floating tank: wide and deep, it comfortably holds four passengers and still rides high over the water. It is eighty pounds of the same aluminum that built fighter planes of World War II. If you dropped one from several stories high, a Grumman would likely suffer no worse injury than a few dents and scratches, perhaps a lost rivet if angled just so. On the calmest days, its bow cuts the water like scissors through silk. On windy ones, the aluminum slices the waves like a silver sharpened sword. Still, though I would trust it farther than any canoe, even a Grumman does not grant a free and effortless ride wherever I wish to go. I remember this each time I visit the Low Lake bog in the Superior National Forest of Minnesota.

The bog sits along the western edge of Low Lake, barely noticeable from the lake proper. It is well guarded, hidden behind turrets of sweet gale and reeds. A moat of water shields and bullhead lilies spreads between the bog and the body of the lake. The layers of protection surprise me each time I paddle through. After the smooth open lake water, the lilies startle you with gentle resistance, dozens of them pulling softly at the canoe's shell, like so many little hands tugging at your fingers. As you press toward the bog, the pads make a steady hollow scraping sound against the canoe's aluminum. Slimy stems catch on your paddle; sometimes they slow your pace so much you wonder whether you are in motion or suspended in a twilight zone of paralysis, poised forever under the sweaty July sun, always halfway between the lake and the bog's edge.

Once you at last carve a path for yourself through the mass, you face the question of where to land the canoe. Along the shoreline, if you can call it a shore, an endless curtain of reeds hides the bog from the lilies. Cattail and shrubby sweet gale flirt with you, luring you into a likely inlet, only to block you with a second line of defense and no ground whatsoever to disembark. You're left to awkwardly back your canoe out into the lilies and seek another option. After ten minutes of searching, you find a break in the reeds deep enough to penetrate to the bog. There will be little room when you land—just a thin space to pull up the canoe and a patch of mucky soil to stand upon. The ooze is too thick to let the canoe slip away, so you needn't pull it far.

As if he had been poured
in tar, he lies
on a pile of turf
and seems to weep
the black river of himself...

They found a man, a tanned and dried-up man in a Danish bog. The Grauballe Man, they call him, for the village near his burial site. Like any other mummy, he doesn't look quite like a person you would recognize. No living human's skin is that texture, no person's head that distorted shape. Grauballe Man is formed like us, but he is not like us; he comes from a world and traditions with which we cannot entirely empathize. Which is why we can place him in a museum as though he were any other Iron Age relic, like a sword or a pestle or a drum.

Yet Grauballe Man was not always some primitive alien artifact. After many CT scans and meticulous examinations, scientists deduced rudimentary information about the man as well as the mummy. They now know how he died (cut to the throat), what he ate for his last meal (gruel from corn). Still—what does that really tell you about Grauballe Man's life, of the bog peoples' history, of their world?

To humankind, these Others are purveyors of secrets... inhabiting their own cultures and displaying their own rituals, never wholly fathomable.
David Abram, "The Ecology of Magic"

In a locked filing cabinet in the corner of my childhood bedroom, I keep my secrets. Every journal, every half-written story, every letter for nobody's eyes but mine, I keep in that cabinet. It is buried under a sheet of picture frames and useless trinkets that I want to neither discard nor keep. Rarely do I open the thing, and even more rarely do I read the papers that live inside. The cabinet's presence is both comforting and disconcerting, for it contains the scraps of my past selves, the remnants of things I used to want and people I used to be.

The bog, like the cabinet, is fiercely jealous of its past. The tamaracks scattered here and there are youthful and feathery-looking, like mischievous bog fairies waiting for you to turn your back so they can scamper away. The sphagnum moss that coats the bog's surface looks welcoming and soft. You can wriggle your fingers down into it and it gives way without much fuss, letting you divide and pick it apart to hunt what you will beneath its surface. The bog is as unassuming a place as you'll find in the Northwoods.

It is a trickster.

Dig your fingers deeper into the sphagnum, past a hand length, and it becomes a tangled and hostile mass, forbidding you to continue. The roots of the moss and shrubs twist tighter and tighter together, ever more resistant to separation. Even with a machete, you can scarcely cut deeper than a foot.

It seems excessive, this unyielding wall of moss, but the bog has secrets of its own. Layered thick beneath the sphagnum is the peat that makes up the bog's base. Preserved within it lies a conglomerate of ancient seeds, pollen, insects, plants, a record of things that were once alive there, but now are not. That bog you are standing upon might be eight, nine, ten thousand years old. The peat binds up all of the centuries it has seen—plants that grew here, nutrients it stored but never used, perhaps a corpse from some ancient civilization, mummified and preserved alongside the rest of the bog's annals. We will not know unless we shovel out the peat inch by inch, unraveling the history the bog labored so long to stitch together. Whether or not we investigate depends upon our respect for the bog's secrecy. It guards its treasure so closely: it warns us not to seek a key to its cabinet of secrets, replacing locked drawers with layers of lilies, reeds, and moss.

We tend to disregard such wishes if they do not come from another living human, and even then we are a species of snoopers. But I wonder if everything, living or dead, human or otherwise, does not deserve privacy if it so desires. Historians found the personal journals of a Puritan minister, Michael Wigglesworth. Wigglesworth writes in code of his torment over his sexual attraction to other men and his terror that someone might discover him. Several centuries have passed since Wigglesworth's death, so perhaps it no longer matters, yet I cannot help but think of Wigglesworth's horror if he knew his journals would be cracked for anyone to read. How long do the dead have a claim on their secrets, before those are unearthed for the greater good of the species? Certainly Wigglesworth's story has value for anyone who has struggled with sexual identity, and it serves a purpose in amassing the buried history of homosexuality. Still, does he have a right to have his secrets remain so? Does the bog have a right to remain at peace and undisturbed? Neither Wigglesworth nor the bog speaks a language we understand, and we interpret that as license to do as we will with their stories. But I think we might consider that a voice is not necessarily silent nor worthy of dismissal if not does not come from a human body. And it is possible that because a secret exists, there is no law that says we must expose it.

This ground is not prepared for you. Is it not enough that I smile in the valleys? I have never made this soil for thy feet, this air for thy breathing, these rocks for thy neighbors...
Henry David Thoreau, "The Maine Woods"

I grew up hiking the conifer forests of the Pacific Northwest. The trails are safe, carefully constructed tunnels of open space in an otherwise impassable fortress of woods. The forest simultaneously delights and silences your eyes. It teases you with explosions of green, yet forbids you from seeing further than a few feet ahead. Only occasionally does the trail deposit you at a stream or an open bluff, where in any direction you see endless miles of forested hills.

I like an outdoors made of trees, one that sucks you in and envelopes you so utterly that you cannot tell where it begins or ends. The bog—the bog leaves me awkward and exposed. Looking across the bog is like a free fall with nothing to break it. The bog radiates outward from wherever you stand with nothing to rein in your eyes. Like a desert, its plants are short and shrubby; acres of moss stretch beneath them like so much sand. The few scattered trees are half-hearted about their existence: the tamaracks are short and fluffy-looking, like they do not take seriously this survival business, and the spruces appear haphazard and scatter-brained, as though they became so absorbed in outgrowing the tamaracks, they forgot details like branches or bark that adheres to the trunk. To stand in the Pacific forests is to be dwarfed by trees fifteen times your height, so thick and dense they can swallow you and never leave a trace. In the bog you are a giant, garish and absurd. Here you are the singular thing that dwarfs all else, the piece that does not belong.

In the backwoods of Mount Hood in Oregon, there lives a crazy old man and his dog. The man is called Larry, and he has lived on the mountain for nearly twenty years, hiding from the rest of the world. Neighbors are scarce, but a woman named Wendy lives with her husband in their own little cabin near Larry's hut. Wendy is one of few people to have met Larry in recent years. She came upon him on the narrow gravel road that winds through the forest near her house. He stood with his dog at his side, head bent back as he strained to see the top of a Douglas fir that had confused itself for a skyscraper. When Wendy called out to him, Larry froze, like a deer that has just spied a wolf. He seized his dog and vanished into the forest so quickly she wondered if he was ever there.

I cannot say who Larry is or why he hides. Even if I could, I would be sure to lose something important. It feels arrogant and rash to mention Larry at all, this man I have not met. I can only say the forest absorbs him like peat around a body. He keeps his secrets close to him. Like the Grauballe Man, Larry harbors stories no one will ever know. I cannot speak to his character, his sufferings or joys, how he feeds himself and with what money. But like the cavern in *The Arabian Nights*, the forest opens to a password only he knows. Behind its initial unyielding layer of trees, the woods unfold another layer, and behind that another, admitting this man's entry and concealing him, on and on and on and on.

The bog, it is no place for a person to hide; it wants not you nor me nor Larry to walk upon it. From any single point you can see all the sphagnum, pitcher plant, bog laurel rolled out in a strange and intricate tapestry—and yet, though you see all at once, you see nothing at all. With years of reading, you might begin to understand how the bog community interlocks and interweaves together, and with the sharpest of spades you might extract a bit of peat to examine. But the bog will never embrace you as the forest might. The sweet gale will still scratch irritably at your ankles; the moss will still shrink away from where you stand; the bog will still send you unsuspecting into a hidden two-foot pool of water. It wants you out.

Both forest and bog ask you to consider your decision to be outside and to immerse yourself in their respective universes. Each time you run into a fallen tree or a hidden pool of water—consider. Each time you break away branches to bushwhack or wrench your foot from a sucking wet bunch of moss—consider.

Yet should you possess the wit and the gumption to continue, the forest will accept you, shelter you, even hide you for an hour, a day, a decade. In the bog you will not find shelter. In the bog, the only people who hide are people who did not bury themselves in the wilderness but who were buried, the ones dead and vanished these many years.

...The grain of his wrists
is like bog oak,
the ball of his heel
like a basalt egg.
His instep has shrunk
cold as a swan's foot
or a wet swamp root...

He grew up in a village some miles from what is now Grauballe, Denmark. Like any other boy, he learned to fight and hunt early, and he threw a spear farther, dodged a blow quicker than far more experienced warriors. He fought his first battle at fifteen, a minor skirmish with a neighboring tribe, and there began his reputation for great prowess on the battlefield. Where he walked, men envied and admired him and women eyed and flirted with him. That era too came to an end, though, when some years later he lost his footing in battle and was taken prisoner. The people sought a sacrifice to secure the land's fertility, and finding themselves in possession of a warrior strong and much-renowned, they chose him. They cut his throat, buried him the bog, and prayed for a strong harvest.

Alternatively:

He grew up a skinny, soft-spoken child who tried to avoid spears and trouble, and he was usually good at it. One evening, when he was nineteen he came upon a man in the forest with a pretty young woman. Thin and quiet though he was, he stopped the man raping her. He paid in knocked-out front teeth, two broken ribs, and—three nights later—a cut to the throat as he walked through the forest. His parents buried him in the bog, where he might rest in honor. His killer was put to death.

Alternatively:

He was married, had a farm, a wife, three children, a dog. He'd had a disagreement with a neighbor over property, and though he meant to have a rational discussion, the argument grew heated and they exchanged insults and punches he never intended. Some evenings later, as he returned from the fields, the neighbor attacked him and buried the body in the bog. No one ever knew what had happened, and though many had their suspicions, the body went undiscovered and the neighbor went on with his life.

Alternatively:

He grew up an ordinary child, neither exceptionally intelligent nor stupid, a boy without any particular skills. He practiced fighting; he tried his hand at farming, without great success or failure at either activity. When he was sixteen, he fell in love with a pretty girl with bright teeth and yellow hair. He grew angry when she turned him down, and one night found her walking alone and raped her. The villagers cut his throat in punishment. They buried him in the bog, where only fools would dare to go.

He is more lone than you can imagine. There is less of substantial thought and fair understanding in him than in the plains where men inhabit. His reason is dispersed and shadowy, more thin and subtile, like the air.
Henry David Thoreau, "The Maine Woods"

I pull at the tips of the sedges as I walk. If I were on solid land, on a road or a trail, I would tug at the wheat-like stems of blue grass that wave at about chest level from the sides of the pathway. I like the burst as the grass releases pods into my hand; I like the roll of grainy beads between my fingers. The bog has nothing in the way of blue grass, of course; the grass depends too much on soil, a steady stream of nutrients, and the disturbance of a road wrenching its way through the forest. The sedges are the only comparable plants that grow in the bog, and so at the sedges I pick. It is a fruitless endeavor: as soon as I've pulled a cluster of sedge tops from their bodies, my palms itch for a new one. The sinews of their stems tear reluctantly, and the edges of the grass chafe at my skin and leave little cuts all along my hand.

The cuts are an exchange. I pay in pain for what you might term stability. I don't mean in the way of balance; you must always be a little unsteady on your feet in the rolling mass of the bog. But as I feel the harsh friction of the sedge in my hand, some corner of my mind exhales a sigh and relaxes momentarily. The sedge lends me a hold on the fact of my existence. Each new blade, each new scratch testifies that I am moving through time and space. The release as the plant yields and detaches from itself proves that I impact whatever is around me, that I occupy a space in the world. Those sedge skeletons I've left strewn across the bog stabilize and ground me. They are a map of places I've traveled, a promise that I was here.

Where is the damn canoe? It did not drift away, I feel certain, but the barrier of shrubs conceals the lake from the bog as well as it does the bog from the lake. My eyes are unused to the bog's landscape, and one patch of bushes looks much the same as the next. I crush clumsily through the shrubs, stepping into secret dips of water, twigs and branches skinning my ankles. My shoes overflowing with water.

The day is blue and bright, and the sun like a sorcerer holds you in a beam of electric heat. Your skin itches painfully as the sun burns it pink, but you forget that too when you step on the bog and feel the water seeping over your ankles and through the pores of your sneakers, like your feet are the Titanic, with the water of doom rushing in. No one even considered the possibility of icebergs. The day is blue, the sun burns, and your shoes breathe water, not air.

It is a morning of gray, and the clouds take turns dropping seeds of water. You will not speak with the bog today. It is beyond you. You bend your face from the sky and press yourself to the wall of your jacket, and like it is a room about to flood. The bottom of the canoe is naked to the rain, and your sneakers, exposed, breathe water like sponges. Never stepping on the bog.

The bog breathes what it wants to breathe. Your feet breathe what it wants them to breathe. Release those tight fists of your whys and hows, your desire for air. Release those fists, if you want to make roads in this place.

...His lips are the ridge
and purse of a mussel,
his spine an eel arrested
under a glisten of mud.
Seamus Heaney, "The Grauballe Man"

He was a young man when they found the body, naked and face down in the peat. That was back in 1952. He wasn't among the original collection of men who discovered it, but he'd been there when the experts arrived to make and give opinions, and he remembered feeling rustic and ignorant in their presence as he clustered with a hoard of other villagers around the body peeking out of a hole in the bog. It had looked unsettling in a way he could never articulate—human-like, but with leathered, folded skin, covered in ooze, and limbs compressed and contorted in ways that no human body should allow. It seemed to occupy the margin between humanity and nature. Nature reclaiming it, year by year, slow like the movement of the continental plates.

He was older now, past seventy, here in this museum with his wife and grown son. Cleansed of bog-slime, encased in glass instead of moss and peat, the body looked tamer, though still twisted and uncomfortable. His muscles ached just to look at it.

His son tried to show him the computer display, but he would have none of it. He preferred the concrete plaque, the newspaper clippings and photographs, or the book one of those experts had written about the bog people. The computer seemed to transport the body and his knowledge of away from the bog, out of his hands, into some pixilated, impermanent, intangible smoke world. He preferred to see the body before him, or to remember it on that day fifty years before. How many times he'd crossed over that bog, as a child and later as a young man; how many times he'd walked right over it and never known—this body that had lain there for centuries, that once farmed the land he used to (before his stroke, before the work became too much). That, he thought, was the way to be buried. Hidden in the bog, his body molded and colored by the land, resting in the place he lived and died. He would change the ending, though. He hoped they would never find him.

Alternatively:

She had dreamed of studying triceratops. The whole paleontologist gig—excavating delicate bones with a toothbrush, arranging them into a skeleton for a dinosaur exhibit, maybe one day finding a new species of triceratops cousin. Bog bodies, even Egyptian mummies, never crossed her mind and would have repulsed her if they had. Now, though, it was different. A good dinosaur skeleton could still capture a piece of her heart and make her swoon with daydreams of their Mesozoic glory—but that was small compared to the Grauballe Man's CT scans. The dinosaurs inspired reverence for their power, but she saw nothing of herself in those skeletons. The Grauballe Man, weird and distorted as he looked, overflowed with tradition and history. He still had hair, for god's sake. They could reconstruct his face, and they extracted his last meal. His last meal! The man hadn't eaten in two thousand years, and here they were, looking at some Iron Age corn, salvaged straight out of his paralyzed digestive tract.

Today was the first time she'd visited the final exhibit at the Mosegård. She'd had to miss the opening day for her brother's wedding, but she dashed back a week later to see it. She felt a little thrill of pride when she saw the crowd. There was a middle-aged couple reading the 1950s newspaper clippings, there a young girl poking at the computer display, there a harried-looking mother and a toddler studying the body. She tried not to get anxious when she saw a group of loud middle-school-aged boys crowded around the case, elbowing each other dangerously close to the glass. She felt protective of the Grauballe Man. Of anyone in the room, she knew best the wounds he'd sustained: his rather shrunken brain, his squashed bones, the damage the Danish farmers had inflicted upon his head with their spades when they first happened upon him. She watched as a rather snappish man stalked in from the next room and barked at the boys to get moving—evidently they had gotten separated from a school group—and they shuffled away, snickering. She exhaled a little in relief and bathed in her pride and tingling excitement.

Alternatively:

She didn't like to look at the body; it gave her goose bumps, and she could already imagine the mummified monsters that would haunt her sleep in the weeks after she saw the exhibit. Still, for reasons she could not express, she couldn't quite pull herself away, and long after her parents have moved to other rooms in the museum, she remained with the body, punching at the computer touch-screen, sneaking glances at the corpse the ways she might at a large and hairy spider.

The screen read A WELL-PRESERVED HUMAN BEING in block letters across the top, and below that was a menu of categories, the body divided up into sections like one of her textbooks. Hands and feet; Bones and fractures; Hair and beard; Teeth. There was a section for viewing the body's genitalia as well, which in a spurt of curiosity she had started to look at, but then an old man walked past her to see the body in the case, in plain view of the screen. She blushed vibrant pink and returned hastily to the main page. Now she stayed safely on the Head and throat-wound section.

The computer offered a facial reconstruction of the bog man, but she didn't think it looked very reasonable. It was human, certainly, but it looked caveman-like and foreign, and when she tried to match the image onto an actual human face, it didn't work. She knew it was a person's body next to her, but she could not seem to stretch her imagination to see it so. The body on the screen was too segmented and compartmentalized, the body in case too leathery and compressed. Less a person, more like a museum she'd visited in New York, where she wandered through vast rooms of dinosaurs and saber-toothed tigers and read about their bones and feeding habits. Even so, it was a long time before she left the exhibit, and in years to come she would get a creeping feeling in her back when she remembered the body or walked through old cemeteries, like there was someone there she could never see.

The quality of cranes lies ... as yet beyond the reach of words.
Aldo Leopold, "Marshland Elegy"

I do not know how to describe the wind. I know the ways people attempt to interpret it—the wind whispers; whistles; rustles; howls. And as I listen to the wind in the pines, I cannot help but feel those words are flat, that, jealous of the wind's spirit, they reduce it to their own two-dimensional, ink-and-paper level. The real wind has more story than any two syllables can capture. Its eerie sound makes me look back over my shoulder as I walk, something I cannot see moving behind me, the trees passing knowledge only they can know.

But for the wind, the bog is mostly silent. Sound creeps in from the forest beyond—the weird fluty notes of a hermit thrush, or the swirling wheel of a yellowthroat's song. In the bog itself, the wind holds a monopoly on sound, seeking a non-existent tree to encircle. If the bog has a sound, it is the wind, and I cannot describe it.

Language does not always fail. The bog may be mysterious, but beautiful words move something equally unknowable within our human cores. Poets and speakers link us momentarily with other people, and our souls shudder with passion and agony. Still, for all its bewitching twists and sparkling power, language is a uniquely human innovation, and we are a lonely species. Nothing else on the planet writes, or even speaks, language the way we conceive of it. Writing is an exclusively human-to-human interaction, and the more entrenched we become in written language, the more entrenched we become in a human construction of the universe.

I hit the hardness of this reality like a slab of iron as I sit to write about the Low Lake bog. The bog is a fantastic, exacting entity unto itself, and to attempt to write honestly about it feels like wrestling the wind overhead into letters and phrases. Today I want to talk about carnivorous plants. There are at least three species in a northern Minnesota bog: pitcher plant (*Sarreacenia purpurea*), with its voluptuous red-and-green cup curving seductively outward, luring unsuspecting insects with a trail of nectar; round-leaved sundew (*Drosera rotundifolia*), dainty and quiet, blending in with the sphagnum moss all around as it waits for ants to march
over it and get caught on its sticky bud; bladderwort (*Utricularia vulgaris*), bright and buttercup-colored, sucking up microscopic organisms from the water as it waits.

As David Abram writes, "we cannot, as humans, precisely experience the living sensations of another form." How do I write about the pitcher plant when I haven't the first idea about its living sensations? How do I write about the ant fallen into the plant's digestive pool when I know nothing of the sensation and knowledge the ant carries in its constant quest for food? I am too aware that the moss keeps hidden history beneath my feet, that the wind sneaks secrets through the air just above my head. It does not whisper, nor whistle, nor rustle, nor howl, but still it speaks in some language I cannot explain. I am a creature of human words, and the bog and the wind cast these off easily, like water from an oily loon feather. From where I stand in the bog, words are not enough.

In Exile On Violet

My parents' car was revving at the curb. I was lugging my duffel down the garlanded hallway of my grandparents' house, when Joyce took my arm, led me to the kitchen, and explained that my sister and I would not be returning home. For one whole week! Joyce (otherwise known as my mother) delivered this news with the syrupy excitement of an infomercial. But wait—there's more! She pointed out how my grandmother would spoil me and how I'd be a big help to my grandfather, as she slipped my duffel from my shoulder and set it on the kitchen floor.

I couldn't smile. I collected the facts: my grandmother and sister had been AWOL all morning; my grandfather was nestled with cancer on the sofa; and the way my mother tousled my hair and winked me to death didn't match her rigid demeanor. Besides, her lipstick was colored outside the lines, her hair acted like it was still in bed.

Joyce got a sudden tremor in her voice. She said she or my father—they didn't know which one yet—would be back in a week to pick us up. She turned and whipped through the den to hug my grandfather goodbye, before bolting down the front steps and into the car at the curb. Bart (aka Dad) waved, unsmiling, from the driver's seat. Puffs of exhaust hit the December air, trailing them like a ghost down Violet Street.

It was noon, day after Christmas, I was still in my bare feet.

Here I am—almost shaving!—and as if my voice hadn't changed or anything I started to think of the cartoons I used to watch as a kid. Not the popular ones with Daffy or Sylvester or Tweety or Bugs. I'm talking about the ones starring no one in particular, where an unwanted newborn is abandoned on someone's doorstep. Lullaby music plays, a sure sign that the baby's future with the new family will be safe and secure and tons better than with the morons who dumped him. Tha-tha-tha that's all, folks!

I closed the front door and slipped my cold feet into brown shag. I retreated to the living room and there, as if scolding me, the Christmas tree loomed. Scattered in its skirts were board games and puzzles and books, still not packed for the ride home, as if they knew all along we were staying put.

It hit me: my sister Danielle had already been told of our weeklong exile. I recalled her and my grandmother's early escape. I'd listened from bed, drifting between dreams and details, as they hustled down the hall and out the door to hit the mall, to buy joy with their crisp Christmas money.

I could see Bart and Joyce gunning down Violet, and at the bottom of the hill, at the blind curve, they brake and skid and hit the oncoming car—my grandmother's car. The screech and crunch busts your eardrums. Bloodied bodies land in lounge-like poses. Sprawled on the hood. Curled under the windshield. Bunched in the floorboard. Mouths agape like movie stars posing for pictures. Cops at the scene throw up their lunch. Hi-lair-ee-ous.

Watch me play under the Christmas tree. Goo-goo ga-ga. Like I'm a friggin' baby. Who cares? Makes me wish for Christmases past. Opening gifts and playing in pajamas, sunrise to sundown, until my father announces that it's time to go to bed because December 25th is O-V-E-R. He used to say stuff like that with a wink, like he was Mr. Brady and I was little Bobby.

But no winks this year. This year Bart gathered his gifts, still wrapped in paper and bows, and carried them to the car, mumbling something about how he'd open them later. Joyce had unwrapped her gifts with the same tedium she applied to opening a utility bill. My grandfather—with his monster milky eyes—exploded with a cough every second to remind us he was still kicking. Danielle and my grandmother cackled at every present like parrots in a gaudy jungle. Phonies. Freaks. Retards.

A rattling cough came from the dark den, shaking me from the memory of yesterday's Christmas fiasco.
An arched doorway connected the two rooms, a demarcation between sun and shade.

I tiptoed to the doorway and adjusted my eyes. Pine paneling, droopy-leafed ferns, console TV. Paw Paw's room. Alter-ego to the living room's gilded cage. He was sitting up on the green sofa, with his feet on the floor, and his head bowed, his mouth ajar. He gripped the cushions, concentrating on his next breath.

The TV got my attention. People were cheering and yelling—it was some sort of movie. A woman skier was slaloming down a hill. She was rounding the last orange flag, the finish line in sight at the bottom of the mountain.

My grandfather exploded with a second cough.

The skier suddenly snapped a pole, sliced between some trees, and sailed over a raggedy cliff. Her arms and legs flapped crazily in slow motion. She landed all screwy like a tossed puppet. It took a moment for me to realize it wasn't my grandfather's phlegmy eruption that caused her accident in some sort of real-life-TV-time-warp.

The camera angle switched to her point of view, like they sometimes do in movies to put you in the character's shoes, and now you, the viewer, were looking up into her friends' eyes as they bent over her. Suddenly all of their cries and questions, even the weepy violins, cut to quiet. The skier heard nothing.

At once I heard my grandfather wheeze. When he inhaled his breathing knocked and pinged and gurgled and whined in the way Bart's car sometimes struggled to make a steep hill. Then my grandfather's exhale tumbled over moist stones and muddy potholes, down into a mucousy low-water-crossing cough.

He made me all queasy, but I sidled up to the sofa and carefully patted him on the back. From this angle I saw his scrawny neck disappear into his baggy blue pajamas. He stretched for a white Styrofoam cup on the side table and spit into it. That's when the stench hit me, as if his extended reach had burst open a pus-filled sore: Paw Paw reeked like the PE showers at school. Armpits and buttholes and jock straps and feet.

I wondered when Danielle and my grandmother might return. I imagined the two of them scurrying through the mall like mice through a well-learned maze, carrying crisp paper sacks of pink and blue and green.

I escaped to the kitchen and inhaled the stirred odor of burning coffee and dish soap. Still on the floor, right where Joyce had put it, was my packed duffel. Going nowhere.

I kicked it hard. I poured a glass of water for my grandfather.

"Thank you, son," said Paw Paw. He swallowed the liquid in long gulps.

He handed the empty glass back to me, and I set it next to the white Styrofoam cup. When I sat on the floor in front of the TV his eyes floated in my direction. He smiled and exposed yellow teeth. It was weird. I was weird. I didn't smile back. I mean, this bony antique was a stranger to me. See, before cancer reduced him to gristle, he used to live life in two solitary ways: 1) dressed in his orange jumpsuit smoking Marlboro Reds in the tool corner of the garage, or 2) poring over the yellow receipts at his Western Auto store he ran with my grandmother. Know what else? In his pre-cancer days he looked like Johnny Carson. Spitting image. There, behind the desk in his office at the Western Auto. I half expected Ed McMahon to be sitting next to him with that drunken laugh. Only thing was, Paw Paw didn't possess any Johnny Carson charm, the kind of charm that made people want to sit next to you and talk.

But he had one thing going for him—the toy aisle in his Western Auto. When I was a tiny kid I'd open games in the middle of the aisle and play. Customers had to tightrope around me to get to the fan belts and spark plugs and batteries. I'd grab a game—Battleship or Sorry or Trouble or Risk—and play with friends who assembled around the board in my imagination. I won every time.

I never understood why toys were in a Western Auto, until one weekend, on another visit to my grandparents, I heard Joyce bitching to Bart about my grandmother's need to spoil. Maw Maw added the toy aisle to ingratiate herself to her grandchildren. Sounded to me like Joyce was jealous.

You know, the odd thing about Paw Paw was that he only said one kind thing to me—ever. Don't get me wrong: he wasn't mean or anything. He didn't kick or curse. He just never knew that I was there. Paw Paw kept in his world, and we all kept in ours.

Except, this one time when he complimented me, it was during the year that Joyce got the brilliant idea to sign me up for the Arkansas Boys' Choir. To show off my beautiful voice, she told me in a rare moment of motherly goo. And the crazy thing is, we recorded an album of choral music! I and fifty other boy sopranos sang in a professional studio. I gave the album as a gift that Christmas, and my grandmother ripped opened the cellophaned sleeve. A singer like Barry Manilow! She admired the pictures on the back (none of which I was in) before putting the grooved disc under the stereo needle. There we were. Joyce and Bart and Maw Maw and Paw Paw and me, even Danielle, sitting around the living room, picture perfect, like we were the President and his family at the White House. Three songs into the album Paw Paw lumbered towards me, dressed in his orange jump suit, and said something about how proud he was, before he left to keep his tools company.

I knew right then I'd accomplished something.

The girl on TV caught my attention. She was crying now. She was out of her ski outfit and into a hospital gown drenched with tears. Her mouth was an agonizing oval as doctors told her she was paralyzed from the neck down. A guy was there, too. Her boyfriend? I focused on the boyfriend's concrete jaw, tight sweater, football shoulders. Beneath his Superman hair he shed a tear with an earthquake lip.

"You look like your dad," Paw Paw said, out of the blue.

From my spot on the carpet I turned and looked him in the face. His thin mouth held no expression, yet his eyes now seemed alive.

"How you sit Indian-style. Watching TV. Just like him."

His voice was soft, like he was testing it out, like it'd hardly been abused by cigarettes. And the remarkable thing was, it was clear, no wheeze.

"You should be running around outside, not stuck here with a sick old man," he added, louder, over the TV. "Stuck here while your mom and dad go figure things out." He exhaled a long, heavy sigh. "I wish to God they could be happy."

He said this last part as if he was deeply hurt.

Then I understood why Danielle and I had been abandoned. Joyce and Bart were on the skids. Over the last year they'd become invisible, huddled on the other side of doors, mumbling and shuffling and whispering like ghosts. And whenever they emerged their averted eyes revealed how they longed to be, I don't know, somewhere else. Anywhere else.

Odd thing is, I turned invisible during this time too. Oh, I was still there—I was always at the house—and yet not there. I hid in my imagination. Know what I mean? If you've ever been a kid you get it.

"I've seen a lot," Paw Paw said, randomly. "That's what old folks say when they get to be my age. I've never seen war—on account of my weak heart—still, I saw plenty of troubles. There are battlefields at home, too. Droughts. Floods. Broken farm equipment. You name it. These hands got me through."

He held them up, shaky and all; he was admiring them, you could tell. He returned them to his lap.

"It's how I met Alice. My first wife. Her daddy's John Deere broke down and he hired me to come to his place to fix it. After a while I became a regular. Alice sweet-talked me, thinking I could fix her, too.

She thought these hands could take her to Little Rock, where life was happening. But no, they wanted to stay—they brought in the money, see—so I listened to my hands and she listened to her dreams or whatever you call it. She took herself to Little Rock and let my hands be. Divorce was blasphemy back then. Devil's work. See—I had this school buddy, his mom and dad divorced. You'da thought the town come unglued. Can't remember his name or his dad's, but I remember his momma. Ever'body remembered her. She'd walk to the courthouse smoking a cigarette. She advertised the crack in her cleavage. A boy's imagination run wild. What a commotion...what a commotion...But Alice wasn't that way. When she and I quit she just disappeared to Little Rock and some judge granted a quickie. Like none of it happened... Still—it lingers in my head. Not love for her. I love your Maw Maw, the only woman I ever truly loved. But memories don't quit, son. Like elephants. Elephants forget nothing. I learned that from a teacher way back. Don't know how she got inside an elephant's brain but I take it as gospel cause it's the same with me."

Alice? Who was Alice? Before Maw Maw there was Alice? My grandfather was divorced? I waited for the punch line...I thought maybe he was fibbing. But he spoke so naturally, honestly. It's like he trusted me with the truth. A family secret. A secret maybe even Danielle didn't know! My sister who knew everything about everyone and bragged about it forever. Such a smart ass.

A cough began to boil in his throat. All that talking had dislodged congestion in his chest. Paw Paw gripped the sofa and spread his legs and planted his feet and gave it a heave-ho. He hacked to a sickly rhythm. He shifted and shuddered and dredged up a prize-winning oyster.

He rested for a long moment.

He stretched for the Styrofoam cup and spit. Paw Paw returned the cup to the side table and settled back on the sofa and that's when I saw that something had fallen out of the hole in the crotch of his pajamas.

"That was Alice coming back to haunt me," he chuckled. "Don't tell your Maw Maw I said that."

His...thing. His Thing! Holy crap. Paw Paw's thing was jumbled in a mound pouring from his pants.

"It's not what life throws at ya that affects ya," he said, "but how you deal with it. Divorce ain't easy, son. Not on nobody. Maw Maw's all tore up. Your dad's her son, but your mom is like a daughter to her."

His mouth moved but all I heard was the voice in my head: "Put your thing back in your pants!" How could he not know it was hanging out? The entire world could see it!

"No telling why things happen, son. Some fall out of love as quick as they fall in. Some it don't matter how much they try, the machine won't work for 'em. Like farm equipment—and Alice. Sometimes it's broke and can't be fixed."

It was long and corrugated like the rubbery hose on Joyce's vacuum. And hairy. Brownish gray. None of it looked like it belonged to him.

"Things happen that's hard to look past. People don't mean to hurt one another. Just happens."

None of the penises in PE class looked like this. Not even Justin Mitchell's. And his was the first to hang low, sprout hair, and leave boys in awe. When Justin showered and toweled it swayed heavily like it was one of the sand bags we carried across the gym for exercise. I stole looks in the showers. Not only at Justin, but at all the boys. And you wanna know what's embarrassing? Wanna know what happened when I looked? When I stared it made my penis grow. Which made me all proud because now mine was just as big. Just as big as Justin's was soft. But one day Justin caught me looking and called me a faggot and gayrod and fairy. I was a car wreck on the inside. I answered with a wimpy smile like I could take the joke. I made some excuse that I was thinking about his big sister, who everyone knew had gone to New York to become a model. But that pissed him off more because no one talked about his sister that way. I waited for my swelling to die before I left the showers, and then, as I was dressing, the guys looked at me and sniggered as if Justin had told them. Their eyes took aim and labeled me for what I was.

"Remember, son: your dad loves you. But you gotta be the man of the house, now that he's movin' out."

A man? I wanted to be a man. To smoke like Paw Paw. To cuss like they did on HBO, goddamn it. I wanted to walk down the halls at school and feel like I owned the place. What Justin Mitchell had. I wanted girls to want me, really want me. And if I impressed one of them, just one, then maybe this sick, burning feeling would disappear forever into the beautiful arms of a beautiful girl.

Without warning, Paw Paw shot to his feet. He shuffled quickly to the wall and stopped. Actually, it was more like the wall stopped him. He threw his shoulder into it and leaned against the pine paneling. He looked like a propped up ladder. He scooted down the hall like that. He was crazy. He acted as if he'd done it a thousand times. There he was, with his butt hole stench and swallowing pajamas and quaking hands, with nothing more than a wall for support.

I jumped up and went down the hall, but the bathroom door was already shut. He was a quick old guy.

I gripped the door handle thinking he could use my help, but then I stopped. There was something about that penis stuff that jumbled up my head. It was weird. I don't know. Some things Paw Paw's going to have to do on his own, I figured. He'd made it this far alone, right? I could hear a powerful stream through the door, a horse peeing, and I could tell he was hitting everything just right which was a good thing.

It seemed to me that something, I don't know what, was set in motion. Something was out of the starting gate and I had no control over it. That was the thing. I couldn't stop it any more than that skier could stop falling off that mountain. No more than her arms could stop trying to fly.

Then I got this insane idea. I wanted to tell Paw Paw my secret. What would he say? He was walking around with his penis hanging out! That story about Alice he told, that was personal and private, right? I wanted to tell him something about me.

I wanted to kiss Justin Mitchell. That day in the showers. I was overwhelmed by an inexpressible urge to hold him. I wanted to reward him with something beyond words, with something I knew was right and true.

A truth packed with possibilities. People cheering me on. With me racing to the finish line.

Then a snap. A plunge over a cliff.

I didn't want to be crowded over by classmates, poked and pawed and offered no comfort, only inhuman labels and unspeakable slurs.

And Joyce and Bart. They might look at each other and say, You can have him. No, you. When all they really cared for was Danielle.

I let go of the bathroom door handle. I returned to my place on the carpet.

The girl on TV is smiling a cockeyed smile. She wears make up and a bright blue cable knit sweater and is sitting at a table in a room filled with light. Parallel bars and exercise machines and cushioned mats. A physical therapy room. She looks at her boyfriend giddy and all. Her hair is pretty with a butterfly clip.

Her boyfriend's dimples burst like fireworks. He looks directly into the camera, at me.

On the table in front of his girlfriend is a big white bowl of potato chips. Straining, she slowly lifts her right arm and exposes a balled fist. She stretches out her arm. It floats over the bowl. And as if someone cut an invisible string her fist falls without grace. Cracked chips skitter over the bowl's edge. Her lips purse, her eyes squint, the whole world is concentrated in her fist. A golden strand of hair breaks from the butterfly clip and dangles in the middle of her forehead. The girl makes a complete mess, yet she's unembarrassed. She raises her arm and smiles. In her fist is a single broken potato chip. She holds it out to her boyfriend, like it's some sort of offering, a wedding ring.

Her boyfriend looks sidelong at the empty parallel bars in the corner. On his Superman face is an expression he can't control. His dimples extinguish.

Paw Paw appears at the doorway of the den, wheezing mightily. "Life sometimes gives you lemons," he says, between breaths. "But, hee-hee, if I didn't just get rid of the lemonade." He then leans toward the sofa and tilts forward, slowly. He's in the hands of gravity...and falls...grabbing hold of the sofa arm.

I extend my arms, impulsively, into empty air. Frozen, like I must've thought I could offer some sort of rescue from my place on the floor. If Maw Maw and Danielle had returned at that second they might've joked that I was trying to gather Paw Paw, the TV, the whole room into my arms.

The sobbing on TV pulls me away. The girl is crying. The boyfriend is gone.

A flurry of noise. Paw Paw is back on the sofa, attempting a smile, with his chest heaving and shoulders rising and falling.
The camera backs away. The girl looks at no one. The potato chip falls from her gnarled fist.

With my outstretched arms, I gather my legs to my chest and grasp them tightly. I hold on to myself. I hold on.

Downfall of the Dans: A Comic Opera

Anacrusis

Sit down and await the orchestra. Feet off the seats. Think about an airplane barreling toward the ground. A liner bound for the iceberg. How a silence, when protracted, builds to a pitch of unbearable tension. Imagine three people in the same workplace being summoned to Head Office. The curtain rises to polite applause. Dan Trumpet steps in first. A short staccato, a burst of panic. The boss is holding a hatchet. The orchestra erupts: a stab of flutes, a kick of trumpets. Next goes Dan Horn. Ears held captive in a spectacle of sound. The notes enter a repeating C scale, scoping out the danger with a picky piccolo. And last, in goes Dan Tuba. The orchestra swells in a crescendo of trembling violins and crashing cymbals. Panic takes flight. The airplane crashes, the liner goes kersplash. Panic ascends the scale as the Dans mooch out the office, catching each other's eye, registering that flash of tuneful dread. A pack of gongs get struck. Once. Twice. The Dans turn to face the orchestra, picking shrapnel from their knees. This music will sweep them into torpor, into terror, into oblivion. The silence protracts, building to a pitch of unbearable tension. The Dans storm out. An echo rebounds in the stalls. It sounds once, then twice, then is gone. Feet off the seats. The aria awaits.

C

Dan Trumpet is riffling through his rolodex looking for allies. His introvert nature makes him good backroom material. A useful backbone for thriving dotcom companies needing strong mental support among IT hotshots and whizz-kid number crunchers. It won't be so bad, he thinks, if he can phone up Dan Bassoon at Shepard Tones to ask if there's space for him in his webslinger squad at the

Discrete Business Park. The short sullen girl in the marketing department who gave him a come-hither look last week watches him lug his data cleansing software through the office as colleagues weep and howl.

The worst thing about that fat tart boss of his that is she's so hideous punching her would only make her prettier. It's not like he's bothered. He's only thirty-four and work is bullshit anyway, and it's not as if Jan can't tide him over for a few months, keep the kids fed and that, help him through a bad patch. Work is bullshit anyway. The recession might be in full-swing and there might be no room for Dan Horn, but so what? It's the perfect time to read more books and learn judo and get blotto. He's not worried.

That's it. You're fucked. Introducing Mr. Dan Tuba, the tramp. Have you met Dan Tuba? He raids bins and peels ants off his pants. Then eats them. Then throws up. Then eats them again. You're fucked. Are McDonalds hiring? Is it so hard? "Would you like ketchup with that?" Don't they have ketchup at the tables? Or are you taking it away? What is dignity, anyway? At least McDonalds give you free chips. You're fucked. What now? Breathe. What now? Keep breathing. Go to McDonald's. What, now? No, sell your kidneys first. Yes, now! Go now! Once more—you're fucked.

D

So there were no thriving dotcom companies looking for a backroom backbone. The dotcom companies are content with their thriving workforce of one. Two for the big enchiladas. (Someone to make the coffee.) Turns out that short sullen girl reported him to the Head Office for "lascivious looks" over the printer and his redundancy pay has been suspended. Oh well. He can always phone Dan Oboe at the IT Fixers and get some grunt work humping processors for bigwigs. It won't be so bad, he thinks, if he has to lift some boxes for a while. Get some exercise!

Right. Jan lost her job too. It's not like she's bothered. But she doesn't know he's lost his job too. So he's bothered. And soon she will be. Their adorable son, Tim, isn't bothered. As far as he's concerned Daddy (Dan-o-matic) and Mummy (The Mummy) are fine and nothing

isn't fine. It's all fine, that's the line. There's another line—at the Jobcentre—where mummy and daddy go in the daytime. How hard can it be to find work in a month? It's not like there's, like, no jobs anywhere, is there? Time to reflect. Read Gorillas in the Mist.

McDonalds aren't hiring. Aren't. Bloody. Hiring. Have you met Dan, the retarded tramp? He would like fries with that but can't afford them. Or the burger. Or bap. Do something Dan. Dan the Man. Do something. Don't just sit there biting your nails and licking your wounds. What is lower than McDonalds? Is there anything lower? OK, so. Get up. Go home. Run a bath. Conserve water. Have something to eat. But no treats. This is wartime, and in wartime, we ration. We sit in the dark and await the bombs. The bombs are coming Dan. Do you hear them?

E

♭ Maybe being in the house won't be so bad. He can always interface with the guys on the technocratic information stream and plant his flag in the moonface of progress. Or watch some TV. He now has time to burn. To exercise, revitalize the Dan Trumpet backroom back brain interdependence database, prepare for his sexual harassment lawsuit. It's not as if he was that rough with her in the cupboard that time, and she was asking for it anyway. She's probably envisioning a bankruptcy ruination personality destruction scenario. Well, no time to sit around. Back to pumping dry the data wells!

♭ Time to regroup. It's not like they've lost their house. Yet. I mean, Jan shouldn't have screamed at the benefits officer like that. Or the police officer. But so what? So they won't have any money coming in. They might lose their house, but it's not like they're starving. I mean, he shouldn't have punched the benefits officer. Or the police officer. But who can say, hands up, they've never broken someone's nose by mistake? It's not like Tim saw much. Well, it's not like he joined in. Lucky he was there to give the men a tissue. Little star.

♭ Daniel, are you listening? Or is that wax back in your ears? Didn't you get them syringed last time? Shouldn't you, maybe? Or maybe, it may be you're a fucking twit. Did you really think you could earn money busking? Daniel? Danny, me old mate? Really? You can't even play the ukulele, Daniel. And anyway, you'd think playing opposite the music shop you stole it from would be a foolhardy move. Wouldn't you? The bombs are magnificent, Daniel. When the bombs erupt in your blood it's like an orgasm, isn't it, Daniel? Ever had one of those? ORGASM. Never mind.

F

To his mind, there's nothing rude about surfing the viral netbase on his phone during the trial. Can't sit by and let the progress munchers nab his piece of the commercial pie, can he? He is listening. To parts. He hears his legal aid sum up his good points—courteous, a strong backroom backbone, often genial. He is too busy datalinking with a contingent of Nepalese financiers about a possible dotcom discovery among netbookers. Something is said about a rape and serious offence and a prison sentence. If he drops his shortfall by a quarter, he could make over £10K!

Losing a son wouldn't be that bad. I mean, he'd get him back again. It's like losing a set of keys. Awkward at first, then one day they turn up under a pile of folders. Tim would turn up later, under a pile of folders. I mean, it might even be good to get rid of him for a while. Some breathing space. Not that he wouldn't miss him, but if he was going to prison for stealing a Ford Focus, he could hardly take him along. Could he? He should ask about that. A break from Jan too. Phew.

Daniel, you are dancing into a nervous breakdown. Daniel, you are dancing into a shopping centre in a pair of blue-chequered M&S boxers with the tag still attached singing "The Winner Takes it All." Daniel, you are twatting a police officer with a ukulele and stealing his wallet. Daniel, you are running out the shopping centre into the arms of the law and flailing around like a spinning top and punching policemen in the nostrils and kicking the windows of the car and screaming "The Winner Takes it All." Daniel, you are not a winner, Daniel. You have nothing. Daniel.

G

No laptops permitted in prison cells. How was he supposed to interface? What sort of online back brain functions without a constant chain-link of factoids and datoids? There was nothing to do in here except think. How could he expect to think when he didn't have the proper means: his database?

Solitude wasn't so bad. It's not like there was a hairy rapist in his bunk. There was a hairy man in his bunk, but he was sure he wasn't a rapist. It's not like he asked. But rapists didn't chew their nails like that or mumble about digital interfaces. Or look strangely familiar. Tim was probably fine. I mean, he was probably crying and terrified. But underneath, he'd be fine. He was strong. Well, he wasn't actually strong. He broke down at a dead fly, but he'd survive. Jan was probably OK too, probably having lots of laughs in the women's prison. They probably showered together and had frolics. Might have been nice to go there with her, ha ha. Mealtime soon. Good. He's starving.

Look what happened, Daniel. "So what?" So…can't you see how stupid you are? "You hardly helped." I'm an observer. A commentator, Daniel. "Stop calling me Daniel. It's Dan." Oh, touched a nerve, did I? "All you do is undermine me, and it's driving me insane." Bit late for that, Dan . . . ee-yell. You're already banged up, facing a long sentence. "I'll plead insanity. I don't care anymore." A nihilist now, are we? "Shut up." Take my advice, Dan. Befriend the screws. Do them favours, they'll do you favours. I mean sexual, Dan. Sexual favours. "You want me to screw the screws?" Clue's in the name, Dan. Yell. "Well, maybe you should shut up." Only trying to help . . . "Dan." Yell.

A

That was it. Without a network of opportunities on a suprainformational überbyte global panoramaface there was no reason to exist. How was he supposed to interact with the blankness of silence, how could he cut his slice of progress pie from the cakes of despair? He couldn't. He could not.

He made a friend. The strongest man in the prison, his friend could lift tables above his head while fending off four guards with his toes.

And from the looks of him, this wasn't a boast. Sure, he might have used him as a punching bag a few times, but these were rites of passage, he assumed. He'd made a friend. A friend that threatened to track down Tim and tear out his eyes if he ever let on to the fuckpigs that he was dealing skag in the showers. But a friend, still. He got a discount on skag for keeping his mouth shut and for helping him through the long nights when he needed someone to hold. He missed Jan sometimes. Only sometimes.

Daniel! "I need to sort this out." Daniel! "Things can't go on like this." Daniel! "I mean, look at me. What happened to me? I get fired and have a breakdown." Daniel! "Now I'm in prison. I mean, something has to change." Daniel! "Something in me has to change." Daniel! "But who can help me? Who can I turn to?" Daniel! "Who could possibly help me?" Daniel! "Oh God . . . it's God, isn't it? I knew this day would come!" Daniel! "I have to ask Him for guidance. For too long I've been running from Him." Daniel! "Why did it take me so long to realise this? He's been waiting for me all this time. Waiting for my love, for my soul." Daniiieeeeeeeeeeel!

B

♭ He lives in a disconnected world. A man unplugged. Lost in the mainframe of reality. He was looking at ten years offline, shut in a box of exclusion with no means of accessing vital supplements on the informational matrix. There was nothing left for him to do. Well, one thing.

♭ OK, he misses Jan most of the time. The longing sometimes is atrocious. Good days and bad days. Mainly bad days. Being his friend's sexual bear is hard, degrading work. Still, it keeps the screws off his back. And he'll be reunited with Jan soon. Bet she was having fun.

♭ Why won't you talk to me, Dan? "Lord, I am sorry for what I've done and the life I've led. I hope you can forgive me in time. I'm willing to work with you towards being a better person. Towards a redemption. I've been living a lie for so long and I'm ready to accept you at last." Dan, don't shut me out. "It's this voice in my head that has ruined me and driven me mad, this voice of the Devil. If I can kill him forever, I'll be free, and I can love at last." Listen to yourself, Dan. You sound like a mental patient. "There are two things I want to achieve in life. One is to find a plateau of contentment and humour, the other is to help others like me survive the abyss, to redeem themselves from shame and sin." Oh, for the love of…"God. I'm not asking much. All I ask is that you accept me and perhaps one day I'll be worthy of your love." Oh, for…Dan, you pillock, you ape, you…Daniel…"One day at a time, Lord."

C

Dan fastens his belt around the light and stepped into the noose. He envisions a clear drop-down fast-choke minimum pain-in-death scenario, but a second overview shows a more plausible slow-choke fall-and-break-legs outcome, a less desirable shortfall. But this was a crisis point. He would have to grin and bear it.

Dan steps out the prison cell into a drizzly afternoon. The guards promise it's Thursday and the screws are certain it's Monday, honest. Jan is waiting for him at the gate with Tim. They don't look pleased to see him, but they've been through hell themselves. Not that they're bothered.

Dan kneels at the altar and feels nothing. His conversion in prison had been born of desperation and the need to connect with someone or suffer the humiliation of the Devil. It wasn't a simple case of talking to a priest and spilling his guts and basking in the divine light of redemption. He has to show he was ready to change in actions. He finds the police officer he'd assaulted and tries to apologise, only to have the door slammed in his face. He apologises to the manager of the shopping centre where he suffered his breakdown. He takes himself to his family and apologises for the shame and discomfort he had caused. They turn him away. Having suffered enough he turns to God once more. He feels the need to believe. To keep the Devil behind bars. Breathing in the cool morning air he feels a warmth opening inside him and decides to perform random acts of kindness. They aren't always accepted with good grace (dragging old ladies across the road) but most people are satisfied (with the cash handouts). Although Dan knows won't work again for the next four years, he is content. Edging nearer to peace.

D

He hangs from the light, choosing a long-term unconscious dead-as-a-doornail pushing-up-daisies strategy. He wasn't much good at living outside the digital interface. Whatever awaits him on the other side, he hopes they have broadband access and a coaxial flex adaptor with USB attachment sticks. This is his idea of bliss.

Back home. Pizza in the oven and *The Incredibles* on DVD. Time to steer the reins of domestic life and get back to relaxing and lounging about and not caring very much. Sitting on the sofa with Jan and Tim and heckling the TV. This is his idea of bliss.

He sits in silence and listens to the night noises: the soft whoosh of traffic and the calming trickle of rain. The stillness of things brings him closer to God. He sends a dream of happiness into the night and prays for world salvation. This is his idea of bliss.

Coda

And so, as the curtains fall, the violins strike a haunting lament for figure of Dan hanged in his prison cell. The audience sit, teeth-clenched in sadness, hoping for a happier climax. A foreboding silence. The final flames dying in the plane. The last few bubbles popping on the surface. From the gloom comes a soft piccolo, playing in major key. The curtain rises. This is Dan and Jan's theme. A ten-note ode to the smooth-sailing ship of domestic happiness. There is mild applause as the tone lifts from existential dread to redemptive pleasure. This is confirmed by the rising organ notes, striking a profound chord with the audience whose skin is prickling and whose hearts are thumping. This is Dan's theme. His conversion and complete fulfillment fills the audience with hope. Perhaps there is something to be said for living a pure and simple life. Perhaps what truly makes us happy are the small interactions with the world. Perhaps we can take off again into the skies, set sail on a liner into the sunset. Perhaps if we come together as people, united in love in happiness, we can make a difference. Maybe this feeling will stay with us when we leave the theatre. Perhaps it's a nice sentiment, but more the stuff of fiction than real life. The curtain descends. The show's over.

Independence Day

Fourth of July and apple pie. It's your birthday for the twentieth time. You pile in the car with your two best friends and drive to a lake house. You decide to stop being a vegetarian for just one day (for the third time that week) and eat a pulled pork sandwich with a bunch of adults you don't know. Everyone's there to celebrate Independence Day, and they don't know it's your birthday. You don't care.

You just got back in the country a few days earlier, after spending a month in Greece. They didn't have real ketchup or hamburgers or Dr. Pepper or a drinking age there so for a few weeks you pretended like you weren't American; you weren't who you really are. No one would know any different. You drank wine from water bottles that you bought on street corners because that wasn't illegal and you had self-esteem issues. Right before you left, your ex- boyfriend told all his friends that your thighs were too big, and he only stayed with you so he could use your car. You realize for the first time that you have not yet experienced true, three-dimensional love, the kind of love where someone thinks you're the prettiest girl at the party, and they don't turn away when you fall sleep next to each other.

You drink too much vodka and not enough Coke, but that's okay; it's your birthday. You and your friends decide to wash your hair in the bathtub. You close your eyes under the warm water, scrubbing the grease and alcohol from your face and bangs. In Greece you took a shower every night after drinking, like a strange cleansing ritual; you always left your glasses on.

He arrives at the lake house in the early evening, after you have washed your face and bangs and eaten another pork sandwich. You have been waiting all day for him to come, but you don't tell him that, you just say, "Hey Dude" or something equally as meaningless. He takes a secret shot with you, so you don't have to drink alone. Later that night you fall off the porch into a bush; he laughs and helps you up, but doesn't look at you with those judging eyes that ask: How much have you had to drink and what the hell is your problem?

You put a cigarette out on his cheek, because you turn around too fast and don't realize he's standing so close; the red ember crushes into his skin, leaving behind a pink blister. You're more upset than him because all night he's been calling you darlin', and you keep acting like an idiot. Later that evening everyone falls asleep on the floor, and you find a warm spot where you can lay your head on his shoulder. He's funny and sweet and whispers jokes in your ear as you drift off. Maybe someday he'll be something more, but for now, you're okay with the smell of his clothes, the weight of his head on yours, the rhythmic rising and falling of his chest. He hasn't left yet; he isn't leaving. Maybe he's not like everyone else; maybe this time will be different.

The Parade

I'm by my window in an undershirt and some underwear, standing partially concealed behind my curtains, watching thick white snow flakes tumble down from the cloud dome above. It's a grey day—a wintry warm and misty sort of February day, with a wan light filtering in and the snow flakes melting as they hit the glistening streets below my window. I've got a cup of scalding hot tea in my hands, and I'm holding it up to my pursed lips, blowing a hot steam off the surface, sighing out a thick fog across my glasses. It's early still, just nine or so in the morning, and I've barely finished eating my breakfast. Some cracked toast crumbs and syrupy jam deposits still stick to the plate on the kitchen table behind me, a Saturday newspaper lies desperately abandoned on my counter, unwashed dishes decompose in the sink, and so on and so forth. I'm standing there sipping on my scalding hot tea with my lips like an "O" and I'm watching the scene outside.

The glistening street is full of shivering people. Like ghosts they are there, hundreds of them, all stomping around in mittens and winter coats and ear muffs, stomping their thick-soled winter boots and twitching around to keep themselves warm, most of them smiling or talking foolishly to themselves. I see the men from my neighborhood standing around with their gloves and their beer bellies and their chafed outdoor faces, creamy little wives and children beside them, a dog, perhaps, running around between them. I recognize many of these men and their families from my morning walks around town, or down by the little creek that drenches itself through the neighborhood—men who are off to do the things that they do, like miniature mechanisms: bankers, tradesmen, workmen, and so forth, little predictable mechanisms that spin around in a constant imitation of themselves, performing their functions. They all know me too, at least by sight, and we greet one another as I pass by them on my way to the university, them nodding in their affably gruff and courteous way, and I, bowed little man, my hands clasped fiendishly behind my back, eye them briefly as we pass.

I see them now on the streets with their creamy wives and their milky children, laughing in their gruffly courteous way, shivering and stomping and shouting. Their wives stand with them, delicate little things they are, a mix of old-fashioned and modern, career-bitch or stay-at-home, slick-cut or portly. The wives stand with their men and chat with other wives, or play with the children that scamper among them. It's a family scene, and the children are running off in all directions, wide gap-toothed grins and oversized winter apparel, hiccups, and boxing one another about the ears, throwing ice chunks at one another, or saying smart things to their Fathers, who stand there leaning against the walls of buildings, nodding grimly, staring away into the mechanisms of their own lives, mumbling something vaguely disheartening in reply.

I stand behind my window, in my room, and watch as everyone stands happily smiling down on the street below. They are all waiting for the carnival parade, an annual costume parade that passes through this town once a year in February, a parade that emerges like a shaggy beast at the east end of town and snakes its way along the streets until it reaches the town center, where it always dissolves again, like soap. It's a costume parade and there's hundreds of costumed townsmen who march through this street as witches and dwarves, who bring candy and confetti and a bit of costumed mayhem to the rest of the crowd. The crowd stands there at the side of the road like a miniature imitation of itself, slap happy and clapping, feeling the moment, as they say, slapping its knees and gurgling with laughter, pointing beefy index fingers at the things that amuse it, and most things amuse it. The parade brings all of these people out of their homes on this early Saturday morning in February, with thick snowflakes kissing them wetly on their foreheads and their cheeks, like cool sweat beads, or a twitch of the nerves maybe, and these people stand there happily together on the street, feeling this sense of anticipation that they are feeling, this tireless anticipation, a tireless waiting for the parade, which is due to pass by here at any moment now, at any moment.

I stand behind my curtain in my undershirt and my underwear, a crumpled little man, holding my half-empty cup of tea in my hands, staring vaguely into the space before me, and thinking. In the distance, I can hear the sounds of the parade, which is already marching towards us from the east end, the sounds of its drums and brass instruments and ear-splitting firecrackers, its individual costumes all singing and yelling and laughing, the unmistakable snap of whirling confetti that cuts through the soft wintry air in papery imprecision. The children can hear it too and they are tugging at the trousers of their majestic Fathers, they are pointing their miniature white fingers towards the east, their eyes and mouths wide open, pushing and toppling one another like the pawns of a crumbling regime, an eager excitement about them. Mothers too are turning towards the eastern end of the street, tousling the unwashed hairs of their children, laughing sagaciously in their earthly feminine wisdom, sharp-cut in suits, or matronly in aprons, until the Fathers too are turning to the eastern side of the street, conceding on this one point, admitting that yes, the parade is indeed coming, and deigning to look over in its direction, these bankers and workmen in their majestic trousers, these little mechanisms that whirl around like mechanical imitations of themselves.

I too am looking, pressing my skin against the cool glass and looking out at an obtuse angle onto the eastern portion of the street, my empty tea cup on the window ledge, my attention fixed on this parade that will arrive here at any moment now, at any moment. From where I stand, I can see a family of four—a man, his wife, and their children—who live in the apartment next to mine and who are outside now and waiting for the parade along with the rest of the town. I know these people well, passing them often as I head up or down on the staircase in our building, they going out, I going in, an exchanged hello or a curt nod, the children shy behind their parental columns, perpetually shy and unknown, maddening toddlers they are, the wife beaming, and the husband talking. He's a banker, a clever sort of portfolio man who went abroad during his undergraduate days, and who found himself and married a beautiful wife, who tiptoes up to my apartment door about three or four times a year and surreptitiously slides a little seasonal greeting card into the mail slot, happy season from your neighbors, that sort of thing, while I in turn send flowers in a paper sheath, with a little note tied tightly around the neck, written hastily and in my childish scrawl, hope all is well, left surreptitiously on their door mat, picked up gingerly by husband or wife at five-thirty in the afternoon, and silently taken inside to be inspected. I know these people well and they know me well, and I see them now as they stand and chat eagerly with themselves and other neighbors from our building, the children dashing about with their playmates.

Suddenly the youngest of their two sons can be seen pointing at the end of the street, pointing and then tugging at the dress of his Mother, shaking the arm of his elder brother, who also begins to point and tug at the legs of his portly, middle-aged Father. The banker and his wife look over, smiling broadly and beaming, proud of their perceptive offspring, and gearing up for the wonderful mayhem of the parade. Others around them are doing the same, children pointing and running, Mothers cooing and laughing, and Fathers smiling with a slight, masculine contempt, though secretly amused like children themselves. For here now is the parade, right here among the people that watch it, a carnival parade that snakes past its spectators like a carpet of strange medieval costumes, witches and wizards, dwarves and wild beasts, strange creatures marching by with their tricks and their candies, passing by the mechanisms that watch them, silently and eerily smiling, like the ghosts from a dream.

The witches walk by first. They all have wooden witch masks with deep set witch eyes and large and crooked hooked noses, with white rag hair, and various shawls and lumpy rags thrown helter-skelter over their hunched and broken frames, witches that cackle quietly to themselves as they shuffle slowly by the crowd. There are scores of these witches and they trudge by in a solemn procession, witches in rags and aprons and pockets filled with spices and things, some even with brooms between their bowed legs, their backs all hunched over and stuffed with pillows, cackling quietly to themselves with modest glee. They walk slowly by the crowd and stop every once in a while to solemnly hand candies to the children that watch them, handing candies to the toddlers that watch wide eyed as these witches approach them, looking mournful and sad with their strange witch masks at the children who laugh and run among them, handing candies to these children and their parents, who pocket them gravely.

I can see the banker and his wife smile happily as their two young sons are approached by a group of three witches. The witches and sons eye one another cautiously, nobody moves for a moment, and then the witches reach deep into their candy sacks and each hand out one or two pieces of candy, patting the boys on the head, who, as soon as the witches depart, laugh and hiccup and fling themselves against the legs of their Father, who laughs in his portly, mechanical way. He too is delighted by these witches, with their solemn progression through the town, and he watches curiously as they pass, pointing his index finger at these things that intrigue him, sweeping his right hand across the panorama of witches as he explains their properties to his invisible wife. She in turn sways back and forth slightly on her boots, sucking on one of her sons' candies, milky white beneath the dim grey morning light, watching the witches pass by her, as the witches walk off strangely and quietly away from her, leaving the people behind them with fistfuls and handfuls of candy, a souvenir for the moment, which has already passed.

The crowd has already forgotten them, for here come dozens of wizards, strange men in solemn blue or fiery red or shimmery green robes and with long white or grey beards, wearing lifelike and impassive wizard masks, their pointy blue or red or even green wizard hats, their gnarled and twisted wizard staffs held proudly before them, walking briskly through the crowd of people that watches them. Everyone points cheerfully as the wizards march by and as they flutter their robes, holding their arms out like wizard prophets, their wizard masks as impassive as ever, their benign wizardry summoning ancient spirits from bygone eras. There are all sorts of wizards, majestic ones in blue, tricky ones in red, shimmery ones in green, and children and adults alike stand in awe as these strange creatures walk by them, offering nothing, walking only by them in their robes and making strange magical gestures in front of them. The banker's children stand there in a mixture of confusion and awe, wanting so badly to ask their Mother about the meaning behind this, behind the wizards' retention of their candy, but they say nothing, and they know nothing.

The people stand by and watch as the wizards continue to march by them and seem almost dismayed at the methodical indifference of them. I watch as the banker's wife turns to her husband with a raised eyebrow, asking no doubt about the candy for the children, and why it wasn't at this very moment being inserted into their pockets. Then, suddenly, as if on cue, and before the banker can reply, the wizards bunch together into a tight cluster and release from them gigantic tufts of colorful confetti, which stream and flutter through the air in millions of papery particles, amidst great cheers from the people, landing upon the scalps and the hair of the people that watch them, the people who laugh and try to evade them, these papery particles, only to be perfectly rained on by them, to be perfectly smothered by thousands of snow-drenched confetti bits, which stick wetly to their wet clothes and to their snow-drenched faces. The confetti crowd cheers and the benign wizards wave and then they too are gone and happily forgotten, leaving behind them only this snow-drenched confetti memory, which clings to the clothes and the faces of the people that stood there and watched them.

I look again at the banker and see a twinkle in his eye as he watches his wife, as if somehow he had predicted all this, this sudden magic from the wizards, and was now taking ownership of this knowledge, right there on the street. I watch as his wife laughs in her delighted, subservient way, and as his children crowd around the majestic legs of their Father, all of them covered in soggy confetti bits, which cling to their hair and their clothes and the skins on their faces. I then see the two children point once more to the east, from whence emerge hundreds of elves and dwarves and gnomes and other woodland creatures, colorful little things in strange garbs, with beards and shiny red noses, who frolic and play with the people that watch them.

The masks of these creatures are all smiling, their smiles are painted on in reckless imitations of the real thing, long stretched out smiles that go from ear to ear in toothy grins and through thick red lips, the eyes so round and recklessly delighted. I watch as these smiling creatures break off from their squadrons alone or into smiling pairs, and as they smilingly grab the hands of children and women, even husbands, as they smilingly lead them around the streets, dancing with them, laughing and hooting and smiling along with them, lulling them into a happy trance. I watch as the banker and his wife look on delighted as two dwarves steal from them their children, leading these children around on the street in a smiling way, clapping and dancing with them in their dwarfish way. I watch as some more smiling dwarves come and surround the two giggling children, lobbing candies and confetti at them, clapping their hands and singing along, as the children cower and giggle between them, happily constrained by the smiling creatures that torment them. The children break free and the dwarves continue to chase them, brandishing now colorful crayons and face-paint markers, waving these like torches, and drawing on the faces of all who are caught by them. I watch as the dwarves reach the confetti-covered banker and his wife, watch as they pause before them and tilt their heads sideways in a smiling, dwarfish confusion, before suddenly taking their faces, and imprinting upon them dozens of paint lines and circles, all over the ears and the eyelids and cheeks of the man and his ugly middle-aged wife, over their white cheeks and eyes, and gruffly over the milky forms of their children. The crowd laughingly attempts to evade these woodland creatures, twisting their bodies to dodge away from them, stepping backwards until they are helplessly pinned against the walls of the buildings and the cars and the others around them, waving their hands—no, no, no—in mock defiance against the smiling creatures that are now smilingly assailing them. The dwarves run around and around and color the town red with their face paint and their markers and they laugh and smile as the people smile and laugh along with them.

Amidst this smiling confusion, a marching band appears and mixes itself into the heaving mass of children and dwarves. The band members are lively and skilled, and they are dressed up as bishops and priests and cardinals and kings, as nobles and intellects, brandishing their brass instruments like rattling sabers, throwing their firecrackers and other noisemakers, mixing the somber sounds of their instruments in with the frenzied cheers of the dwarves, who weave in and out among them, cornering children and parents between them, painting their faces with red face markers, and stuffing thick tufts of wet confetti balls down the collars of the children's shirts.

I watch, and I hear the festivities through the window in front of me, the sounds of individual confetti laughter piercing like paper cuts through the air outside and in through the impassive glass of the window. I listen to the rustle of confetti being flung into sweaters and down shirts, to the soft swish of markers etching strange patterns and designs onto the faces and clothes of the children, smiling to myself at the sounds of the people outside, these people whom I pass on my way to the university each morning, these people I think of while silently reading alone in my study, and who sometimes flutter like ghosts within my thoughts, who whisper mechanical words to me in my thoughts, whispering mechanical words that unnerve me, whose whispering words are like the splintering crashes of glass bottles at night, the slight rift in the air as they are hurled up in swift underhand lobs, and the pop, pop, pop, as they implode on the stone walls of the building I live in, these openly secretive little creatures, who whisper and scurry away from me in my thoughts, leaving me dazed in the middle of the night, sitting up alone in my bed with a warm terror on my brow, and a scream welling out from deep within my lungs, alone there in my bed at the university.

The marching band has passed on and the dwarves continue to smear their paint all over the faces of the people around them. There is something slightly fiendish about these dwarves, something impenetrably ghoulish in the way their smiles are painted on from ear to ear, little men behind dwarf masks, running around as part of this parade. I watch as the banker and his wife and their happy children are surrounded by a group of these dwarves, who close in on them and brandish their felt markers, and who pin the arms of the children behind them, rubbing strange red patterns all over their faces, and then too onto their coats and the sweaters beneath them, tearing open zippers and flinging away buttons, drawing wildly on the clothes of the banker and his giggling family. Everyone smiles in a happy fashion, waving their hands in mock defiance—no, no, no—and struggling feebly to get away, to no avail, being so pinned as they are, so happily pinned back by the costumed creatures that threaten them.

As the dwarves do their work, the snow continues to fall thickly down in flakes that melt in wet smudges on the streets and on the faces they land upon, dissolving the red paint and drenching the confetti, leaving behind a strange red paste, a strange mixture of face paint and drenched confetti bits, which slickers and slides through the hairs of the laughing townsmen, the banker and his wife, and their unknown children. The people use their coat sleeves and their mittens to rub the red paste off their faces, and in the process cause it to smear still more across their faces and across the fabric of their clothes, which stains and absorbs the gooey confetti mess. The scene looks increasingly confused as the crowd blends together into a mass of dwarves and colorful smudges and I peer through the frosted glass of my apartment and see the banker and his family, straining my eyes and just seeing them, for they can only be recognized with difficulty amidst the heaving homogeneous red mass.

The dwarves continue to run and to pounce, and soon they are joined by a new group of costumes, a group of court jesters in asymmetrical outfits and bells on the tips of their hats, who walk through the red mass performing tricks and trickery, and who stop in front of the crowd with wet and grimy dish rags, with smelly rag mops, wiping away the smears of face paint and confetti bits that are stuck to the skins and clothes of the people, and replacing these with a dirty brown mix from their rags, full of grimy scum. The dwarves continue to run around, smearing red paste across the faces of their observers, as the jesters mock scold them with their index fingers, and mix the paint with the dirty brown and smelly refuse of their dish rags. I can see the banker laugh heartily at the scene, nudging his wife and children towards the jesters that approach them, holding his children still as these jesters wipe and re-wipe the color away from them with their grimy, smelly, filthy rags. The children are flailing their arms, wheeling their arms around like windmills, delighting their Father, who laughs and laughs, and amuses himself with the sight of his young sons being mauled and assaulted by the smelly rags of the jesters. The scene becomes increasingly confused, as dirty, muddy rags are wiped and scraped across the townsmen, leaving them brown and dirty, and imbued with a reddish tinge. The banker's wife and children are giggling out in their happy confusion, reeking of dirty dishwater and crusted over with grime, as the filthy banker laughs and laughs mechanically, amused in his portly, mechanical way.

Suddenly, the jesters and dwarves run off, pointing their fingers to the east and hurrying away, their masks still smiling, their eyes showing somehow this palpable hint of smiling fear. They run away and are immediately replaced by a dark mix of brisk-walking black bears and galloping horse-wolves and other strange and dangerous forest animals, which march through the crowd, wielding sticks and stones and even knives, carrying these like frightening weaponry among the dirty people, who in turn laugh and point at them with their long and bony index fingers. The bears and wolves stand supernaturally tall, in majestic woolly black or silvery grey fur, their eyes like impenetrable black marbles, deep set and impenetrable pools of terror, impossible to decipher, a frightening sight to behold. I watch as several black bears approach the banker and his family with stones in their paws, and as they crouch down on all fours to let the children pat and fawn over them. They crouch there patiently, deceptively, looking sometimes at one another as the children's grubby hands paw and fuss all over their fur, and then, after a moment, they rear up suddenly and ferociously on their hind legs, still holding their jagged stones, and then they fling these crazily like glass bottles at people within the crowd, pop, pop, pop, right into the teeth of the people that watch them. The banker and his wife and children cheer and clap, and watch with mock fear as more bears and wolves begin to throw their stones at the crowd, as others wield their sticks and begin to beat the dirty people around them. Still more wield knives and begin to slash at the clothes of the people around them, gashing them apart like gummies, red paint flushing everywhere. The banker himself is approached by a group of wolves with wolfish tongues hanging from their snouts, which tower menacingly above him, and he smiles as he covers his face with his arms, feebly blocking the cuts of the knives that now rain down upon him, these methodical cuts inflicted upon him by the wolves and their unsmiling black eyes. His wife and children are laughing as they watch him get cut, and they in turn cower down on the ground as other bears flick stones and sticks at their fragile little frames, rearing up on their hind legs at full height, they too methodically unsmiling, with their unknowing and terrible black eyes.

The scene grows increasingly surreal, as oversized bears and wolves and other dark and frightening woodland creatures begin to brandish their knives in earnest, slashing and slicing the crowd, which crumbles and falls into a happy red pool onto the street below. I giggle as I watch the scene unfold beneath me, taking hot sips from my scalding hot tea as I stand above in my undershirt and my underwear, awaiting the end. The crowd is cut apart by the knives of the annual parade, gutted and torn to shreds by the gurgling knives of this carnival parade. It lies down and rests on the streets as the parade continues to pummel the people among it, the people whose faces and clothes are now covered in a mixture of confetti and grime and red paint, their guffawing smiles like broken piano keys, ragged and broken little teeth on the glistening street beneath them, their broken bones still laughing mechanically as they flail and crumble beneath the blows. I watch as sticks and stones come crashing through their skulls with a heavy precision, their bodies lying down in a sea of confetti and mud, in a sea of colorful red paint. I watch as the banker is separated from his screaming children and his screaming wife, as he mechanically runs a few yards to escape the knife of a menacing bear, which stands there on its hind legs, eyeing the banker with its impassive and menacing black eyes, only for the banker to run into several more wolves, who fling stones at his head, and then thrash him with sticks to the ground, where they then carve him into a red carnival pulp, which gurgles and spews out red songs from its throat and out of its mouth, and onto the pavement near its battered, broken, mechanical head. It lies there twitching and broken, like an imitation of itself, a mechanical thing that goes round and round, whispering strangely inside my head, like a ghost haunting my thoughts, a ghost I cannot and dare not comprehend.

I stand at my window in my undershirt and my underwear, drinking my tea, watching the street below me. The parade has passed by me and it continues its march towards the center of town. I can hear it pass by the rest of my neighbors and their families, by the other townsmen I pass by each day on my way to the university. I stay a moment longer at my window and watch the thick snowflakes dance down from the grey dome above, keeping my thoughts in a quiet trove within myself, careful to keep them happily and safely inside myself, like tiny mechanical ghosts, which flutter and twitch around the inside of my head. Below me, the streets are silent still, glistening under the dim grey light, awash in a thick mixture of snow-drenched confetti bits, and a smelly, red paste.

These Old Boots of Mine

I can't recollect the T-shirt I wore then, but my jeans were blue and tag-rag. I think she wore jeans and a T-shirt too, or there was a top, a yellow one, to my mind. Altogether she looked a sunny girl and gave me a sparkling smile at any casual meeting.

Then we set off by bus to a remote town to visit her college girl. Summer stretched around and they had holidays. We had to hand some papers to her mate, something urgent and needed, otherwise we wouldn't leave for such a far trip. However there occurred a long summer ahead and she was only eighteen then.

It's amazing but there were some taxis waiting us at the bus station in a borough. Or there occurred some private motorists, possibly. No matter, we could take a car and go straight to her mate in Park Lane. Or it was a Green Street then. But she told me it wasn't proper to do that and announced a desire to look round the town. So we walked down there one waved his hand to. Then she wished to ring up to tell her mate we'd come. No coin box set around to give a call! There was only the long whitewashed fence of a hospital on the way, no office to make a call from.

At last I found something like this, with a national ensign on the house top. Yet we didn't find her college mate at home, she was to come. Leisurely we went on along a dusty street. Behind us the sun shone above the flag, and I was thirsty. The Green Street hided herself at the town outskirts as it had been supposed to. But the street happened to look rather pleasant—a row of newly built cottages with cheerful fences. A booth was set nearby in the trees shade. No one to lounge about, it was too easy to come up and take my beer and cigarettes for her.

Her mate lived in a block of flats, the only one in the street, with several front doors. They had renovation there about the flat, and a serviceman said that they had gone to buy something like a solvent. It strongly smelled of running repairs. We went out and sat down at the entry to have a smoke. We sat there waiting on a bench. The day lasted on, the sun was hanging high above the house root.

…A child was whining somewhere about! From behind the cigarette smoke a thin dismal whimper made its way through. In a summer street it dismayed us. There was somebody whimpering faintly in the midst of the day, at the edge of the hot town. And we were just sitting there smoking comfy, nobody to hinder. And then this needless whine, lonely as the huge block in that still Green Street. Or it was Park Lane? Thin and even, a monotonous whimper came through leisure of a carefree day as a bothersome gadfly throughout the cigarette smoke. One couldn't bear it sitting there. Where did it come from? What was it?

Quietly an old woman whimpered behind a door on the ground floor, we detected her through her scraping. No one to see around! Half-insane, she repeated that they wouldn't have come for three days. It was impossible! She asked us to come over to the window. She knocked the window sash with a thin as if a child's hand. My girl gave her an apple through a ventlight. There was nothing more to do. One was not to smash a door or to break a window! We just went on sitting there and smoking.

Then her college mate came and took the urgent papers. We told her about the mad old woman. Well, her relatives might have gone out to drink themselves drunk in the morning or since the evening. May be, they were gone three days ago, and she might be not insane.
We left there by the last bus. They wouldn't let us board a half empty bus for a booking office closed. Then we quietly took seats stowaway. No tickets to leave the mad world!

The home platform met us with an evening downpour. I thought of autumn to come. We dropped in a department store and I took there my boots then.

Snow Break

Nobody's listening, thinks Noland, the DJ, looking out at snow coming down. Ratings down. Revenues down. Now, though not yet winter, down falls this downy fluff. Some slip of nature? Picture chafes like video snow. Breast-soft tufts land lightly on already six stiff inches standing on the sidewalk and tops of cars parked in the staff lot, traffic in near distance on Armstrong Road (salute to Satchmo) thin and jittery, unsure how to steer in ghostly stuff. L. B. Noland, occluded, watches cars slosh through the snow with wheels churning like loose stones rolled underfoot. Not a soul's tuned in, not even for the weather. He sees himself lost in snow. Double-pane, wall-length studio window behind which he stands, dustless inside dust-proof booth, gives back his pale reflection—frozen—a little leaner lately thanks to long walks at dawn with Eileen (true-blue wife in otherwise touch-and-go life)—regular regime she's become tyrannical about (this morning sky silky, no sign of sprites riding in white)—though image in glass, fading at edges into invisibility, is no longer as brash now green in him wanes. He feels less substantial. (A shadow of his father at same age. Or what Noland earns after years on-air doesn't get him off the ground.) Future has come to this, present bland as blankness he sees. Days slip by as if snowshoeing with just enough movement to keep from freezing, each as difficult to remember as one yard of frozen field from another. World goes by this fish bowl and never sees him going cold.

Eileen, meanwhile, unfolds with intelligence of a flower, something curious and more potent in her. Not since year they spent on a college campus together, before their daughter, Lindsay, was born (herself now pursuing higher education, suspicious of all secondhand reports), when they waked in this sun-sprinkled shoebox, married housing, Eileen's just-ironed hair arrayed on the pillow—a mystical redhead, tips dipped raspberry, green nightie she wore (he recalls) hiked up like green wings…not since that idyllic year has Eileen looked more alluring, more earthy: skin ruddy, hair (webby marvel), eyes changing colors of earth (green-laced brown by lamplight), limbs solid and firm as well-packed soil (that walking) and, as the earth, not flat. He remembers her sweet shape in tattered denim of their generation (stitched red heart patching hole in the crotch) jogging to keep up with his long stride as they headed across the green campus to morning classes. It was his only year, though Eileen went on—and on—now a curator at the city museum three blocks up the street from where they live. These days, except on the golf course, Eileen's earthiness leaves him in the dust.

"Come Together," another oldie from *Richland's GOLD Standard,* resonates over speakers, first bars an echoing reminder of something else lost. Noland checks elapsed time (0:09), length of tune at 4:07 almost a saga in saga-like lives of its singers—though world in present year, as Beatles belt it out, could use more unity, as then—but who the heck's listening?—and he wanders out of studio, thinking of thousands gathering at those yellowing festivals, egos dissolving like snowflakes in salt water. In the hall leading to DNN News, Noland's space, cubicle: dark-blue, cloth-covered partitions with off-white L-shaped desk-top (colors matching present mood and outside world). One deep drawer for his (few) files and roomy storage compartment with light-gray lid and silver latch, which he leaves unlocked. Look if you want. Take. His spirit spins around this small sphere, ends in this whirl-pool. By a long box of cards he uses to program the station's music, a battered IBM Selectric for typing labels, so outdated since everyone—reporters, traffic loggers, copywriters, every other music programmer—have long since left it in dust. Noland silently resists. Works by hand. Wants music to fit like teeth in a zipper, nothing no software can do, like zippy rhythm, TUM-Ti-Ti-TUM TUM of "Zippity Doo Dah."

He catches himself whistling that old Disney tune, thinking bluebirds, spring, as he slides a shallow drawer out from under work surface to take a cigarette from pack resting in the tray for pens and pencils and his colored markers. Red bulls-eye logo stares up—what's his aim?-- ringed with white, olive, black. Lucky Strike Green they were called when his father went to war, then American Tobacco Company donated green dye to military effort and left the pack this frosty white with only a thin ring of olive to remind you of its once distinctive color. "IT'S TOASTED." Lungs smoke-cured— bulls-eye, straight to constricted heart. He's got to give up few he smokes. Will a smokeless self, Eileen's wish. He strolls over to the high window on outside wall to stare at white world. Some longing of his separates as snow.

Caitlin Winfree, sales secretary, tap-taps nimbly in nest of light by her monitor, fingers a blur, though because of stormy weather no sales folks around. It's a skeleton crew onboard. L.B. misses ancient clack of typewriters; where have flower-like Olivetti girls gone? American Dream Machine– "No improper spacing! No shading or ghosting!" Clunky as the Edsel, gone way of 45s, LPs, nickel- in-jukebox. Caitlin's cubicle, open-ended, fronts a cluster of seven where in the wide hallway, a moat around studio with its cinnamon-colored carpet, sales sharks swim. She stops, resting hands on keyboard, nails clipped square and painted assorted colors; her fingers are short and thick as hi-liters in plastic wrap pushed into a corner of her neatly-kept desk.

"Hey, Noland," Caitlin says, swiveling to him. "Got time for a real smoke break?"

Mercurial suddenness of her offer makes him smile— sidelong, sly, but he wordlessly shakes his head and leans an arm along the sill. Birds of passage on a break in their journey, he and Caitlin, nice thought. She's fiddled with tilt cord so blond blinds are flattened to invisibility and lifted bottom rail half up the glass—better to see the snow, which has slowed, flakes like hollowed-out cones. It's a holiday to her. A low line of intricate bushes outside lie like inverted brooms below white whorls of accidental design on the pane. Here he belongs—a rare feeling. Yet he's blue. To look out is to sense cold feet, numbed by atrocity of snow. It saddens him, not as when a kid—falls too thick, snow without laughter, ice moving in too close. As he watches white stuff mount, something cold and repressive settles on his skin, chill of a ghostly presence. An odd parabolic light, gray and transparent, flits across his eyes—or is it just a little shadow running into the field where radio towers stand and losing itself in white? He's taking a break but no break in cover of gray-black clouds over whitened field, transformed so dry stalks by transmitter outbuilding loom yolk-yellow. He's having trouble warming himself up to his show; if inner weather bears a relation to outer, it's just a question of reversing current. But coldness he sees leaves him low with nothing to express.

"Why you here, Caitlin?" He tilts his head to scene outside.

"Catching up. Now that sales staff's gone."

"Better go yourself, snow'll be up to your headlamps."

"Nah, got my truck." She seems restless, yet dreamy. "Goes through anything." Her kelly-green Ranger. It's backed up to the sidewalk leading along front of the building, snow filling its bed, a short chip shot from his Olds, where the lot like undulant skin with milky mounds of their vehicles, oddly blue-veined through snow, narrows into a basin of brush bristled with icicled flakes beneath a thick-et of pines by Armstrong. Wrists firm, he thinks, hands ahead of ball, let the sucker roll to the hole. Eileen's been on him to play less golf, read more. It's an old story between them. She's probably curled on the couch right now catching up on her quarterlies, *Journal of the Institution of Cornwall* or that other one, *Transactions of the Denbighshire Society*, or maybe with weather like today pulling out battered copy of *Wuthering Heights* for twentieth time since they've been married. Snow-laden field would look like a Brontë moor to her, but to him just space, vista on which he'd like to send a golf ball high overhead till white speck splits uprights of distant trees as if tee-off were field goal before disappearing into lactic sky, a perfect melody running through his mind as feet and hands complete follow-through.

"…Come together, right now, over me…"

He sees Eileen with brown-framed reading glasses pouring over a page, curtains pulled aside for this odd early snow, logs crackling in seldom-used fireplace. When last they got an afternoon fire burning between them, L.B. can't remember. Doing morning-drive in Poughkeepsie? A song out at the time, "Afternoon Delight," something they hardly play now—a "lunar," once in a blue moon. "Funch" Eileen tagged their midday trysts. In the morning they're too busy—do their walk—in the evening, too tired. He sleeps with Yes, wakes with No. Same with everybody, reports *USA Today*, last week's "Life" section.

"Sure about that smoke break?" Caitlin says. "We could romp over to the transmitter." From below, by modesty panel of her hutch, she lifts a handbag of red cloth, like a whimsical laundry sack, and loosens drawstring. "Where'd I hide that thing?" she says, searching. Coarse teeth of a comb appear but no compact or other cosmetics except assorted bottles of nail polish, colors blurring with her searching fingers—purple thumb, pink pinky, blood-red of little whiffet she flips bad drivers from behind wheel of her pick-up, green the hopeful forefinger she points to show Noland sales doing better than he thinks ("Why worry, L.B.?"), ring finger of yellow, sunny as her marriage. He stands over her with bag loosely spread on her lap, thinking of dreams he's glibly pared like nails. Pens tumble. A small screwdriver turns up. A "church" key—nowadays what for? Her jostling jingling ring of keys. A torn, clear-plastic blister from a battery pack peeks out, empty, which she tosses in the trash. "Thought I put darn thing in here."

"It's okay, Cait. Don't have much time."

"Believe me, L.B., one puff's all ya need." Caitlin is furry and sweet. Likes sweets. Half a Hershey bar lies on her desk, ripped foil and dark wrapper neatly tucked under; something saved for later. She folds bag closed and looks up with a blank expression on her round face, humid flesh of cheeks and forehead flecked with tiny white nicks—some accident as a child, Caitlin's told him; ran through a just-washed storm window diving after a bouncing ball. Her nose is like—what else?—a button. A month ago she sheared her long, dark hair. Noland was surprised how sexy she looked with cut close to her scalp, almost a stubble like Sinéad O'Conner. Caitlin's not much older than Lindsay; somehow remembers Bee Gees with odd affection, likes Led Zeppelin. Now she's patting herself, looking for mislaid reefer...hip pocket...breast. She's got on a wrinkled denim skirt, bibbed, over an orange sweater with a ragged hole in one elbow. She's short and round—not much beneath bib—but hips curvy. She stands, pat-patting places already checked, then plops into swivel chair.

"Did I leave it in the Ranger?"

"Really, Caitlin. G otta get back to my show."

"Didn't smoke it already, did I?" She stares at her toes. Scuffed Chippewas, laces flapping, fit snugly over red woolen socks. Not fussy about shaving her legs. Or, he's noticed in summer, armpits. "Don't think I did."

She stands again and runs downy hands with pied nails up her body once more, patting, Noland brightening; a laugh bounces of out him, imagining underneath denim-bibbed dress and orange sweater where joint might be.

"What's funny," she says, laughing too, his infectious. You Caitlin, and how Eileen was with nothing gracing her sturdy body but a joint between her lips. What's Winfree like? Eileen, past what's past? A romper. Furry limbs frisky. Here, there—everywhere! On air. How's this? Whee! What bliss! Rock-and-roll, L.B. Tumble, intertwine. Curve of hip, bend of elbow. Twin puffs under arms framed by silky shoulders. Up. Down. Pat. Twinkle of twat. Lips glued to, oh, whatever spot. Knee by ear. Wink of tit. Tripping tomboy, rangy. Dark thatch watching, eye-flower. But first that joint to make it seem forever.

"I know." She sits, hikes skirt and a deep well of denim opens in her lap. "Save yer Lucky, L.B." He's forgotten it, geographies of two women's bodies on his mind. Out of one woolen sock, where it's been lodged inside her boot below stubbled curve of calf, she extracts a thick, perfectly rolled joint, wrapped in a swatch of cellophane. It's shaped exactly like unlit Lucky in his hand. "Let's do this." She flicks off cellophane, cradling reefer in her pale palm.

"Let's see that," he says. Down on haunches, close by her friendly knee, he stares into her lap where her cupped hand rests. Her lap he would nestle into. "It's so fat. Must be a quarter-ounce."

"Suppose so."

"How'd you make it so perfect?" He holds Lucky alongside for comparison. "Like this."

"Jimmy," she says of her husband. "A roller."

"So much though."

"Got a good crop this year."

On a tract of land in Winston County, ten acres split by a rippling stream, Caitlin and Jimmy live in an eighteenth century farmhouse they've restored, dilapidated out-buildings beyond, with two horses named Ed and Juba, three dogs, one actually called Romper, four cats—Tambo is one, he remembers—five chickens, a rooster that responds to Strum, and Puffy the parakeet ("Puffy wanna puff?"), plus an aquarium big as a shark tank of exotic fish they like to sit in front of stoned, listening to electric-blues of Led Zep. L.B. and Eileen have been out to their farm, though they don't grow anything but sinsemillia in a sheltered patch of willows by the creek, among wild strawberries, sweetbriar and honeysuckle. Each spring, Jimmy sows ten to fifteen plants here and there that grow twelve feet high, although harping on TV of America's Drug Tzar, hand slashing air like Carrie Nation's axe as he lashes out against casual user, has scared Jimmy into considering only two or three this spring. Well-hidden.

"Wish I could, Cait. Screws me up. Not on my toes."

"It's all in your head."

"Right. Too self-aware."

"So?"

"So everything on-the-air takes forever."

"I see," she says, dark stubbly head nodding with a fetching childlike glint in her chestnut eyes. "'Riders On the Storm' must take a lifetime."

"Sixty-second spot takes a lifetime."

"Heard one on way home last night after a toke." She scrunches her face, eyelids fluttering. "Girl with that husky voice? 'Now's my time of ripening.'"

"K'mon and Kiss Lingerie?"

"Ran two lifetimes. Thought I'd surprise Jimmy."

Lucky guy.

"See what I mean, Cait. Slows time. Four hours of real airtime—already a long journey in a little room."

"You know it," she says, considering, fingers curled around cigarette-sized reefer. "Like 'Light My Fire.'"

Oh yes. A romper. Eileen when L.B. wasn't stuck doing mid-days. Funch. Lazy loony lingering tumble on an endless day like today with snow falling all afternoon and Eileen in her bo-ho Indian-blouse-days like loose-limbed, furry, roly-poly, cuddly Caitlin with cushy Winfree rump a sweet basket of wild strawberries-rose petals-honeysuckle-sinsemillia in his hands, fragrant hotbed arched in ever-lovin' air! Whole Lotta Love! "Get the Led out!"

"C'mon, Nolie. Quickie behind transmitter. Nobody's there, I swear. Gordon's over in production with a bunch of mikes."

That means Chief Engineer Gordon Fermi will shortly be in the studio replacing smoke-crudded microphones with newly cleaned and refurbished ones. So ticked off, he thundered at a staff meeting like a raiding Indian about jocks and reporters still smoking in the building, not to mention "friggin' studios." Next, banned in the lounge. A crowd behind the transmitter, all kinds of smoke in electric air. L.B. lights the Lucky and takes a long drag from it.

"I'll wait till two. When you're off."

"Can't function on the stuff. Especially day like today. Closings, cancellations. Got to be together."

"Come visit us."

On their last visit Eileen came home with a yellow tabby. It'd be a year old now. Her-she, Lindsay called the cat, but it ran off day she left for school.

"Do a number then, okay?"

"Sure."

"You guys are cool."

"So are you."

"Lindsay's lucky to have cool parents."

And what a lucky stiff Jimmy is!

"Gimme a hit of that Lucky," Caitlin says, secreting perfect joint somewhere on her herbal-scented person.

"All yours," Noland says on the go. "Got to get back to my song I'm running out of."

"Don't forget Eileen when you come."

Eileen? And in glare and silence of unbroken snow, pale as face of death, blue notes spill over in bone-white air. Against backdrop of pines welded to clouds with bellies opaque and being hurried sideways by the wind, whiteness is suspended in a wash of blue. Hell frozen over, curious expression from childhood. Cold as hell, Eileen sometimes says, exhaling white breaths, idiom weirdly at odds with fire and brimstone: Hell like this—unmapped snow, flotsam of fate, cold and unchanging, snow field over-shadowed by radio towers that pierce the sky like pitchforks and in their length cast a pall over the landscape. He might as well be beyond Down Under, day unending, sun a pale disc circling overhead in a weird loop, hour passing into hour without darkness, every object etched in light, in ambivalent white. White as milk. White as Snow White's cheeks, or a good egg. White as suit worn for First Communion, white shirt and white tie, coat and pants, white bucks with pink soles. Everyone in white, girls all white, except shoes, so shiny black against white anklets you could see up, all of them stopped souls in procession before hour of Mass as if caught in a game of freeze tag. L.B. remembers sins of a seven-year-old and how they left him cold. Was anyone listening? Oh my God, I am heartily sorry...He turns to catch his fading song, and that wash of blue breaking in the dense sky broadens above slender screen of pines, a widening crack. Shafts of light settle in long slats along cinnamon carpet—sudden sunlit scudding snow moving Noland like cathedral light as he scuttles into the studio. Synchronicity? Order in world he's unaware of? Who can say how low pine sap has fallen, later to rise and burst through—a future buds in everything, clustered or alone, or waiting to break. Like blossoming of Eileen. Like regenerative heat of funch. This is the life I have made. Hemispheres of his brain drifting apart snap back, come together, as he opens the mike, earthiness of Eileen's body before him and how it leans from earth itself in a gesture of play, homing in. Another land, entered into like hope, and passed through.

Jan LaPerle

New Motorcycle

My friend said she likes a man who looks like he could last
through the winter. She said this over Easter ham as it sat
split open, each of us with a slice on our plates, and sometimes
I pretend my man started his life when we met, and that I know
each of his winters, that there was no grief, sadness, other women.
Other times I watch him carry it all beautifully, pushing along
like a shiny hearse. At my grandfather's funeral my dad said
his dad's coffin was the same color of his new motorcycle.
He said this as he rubbed the coffin like he would have done
at the motorcycle shop, right beside my grandfather's feet,
and just like that grandpa rode off, revved up right there,
kicking up flowers, and burning through the rug.
The fat hung from the Easter ham in strings and chunks, and I fed
most of what was on my plate to the dog under the table.
I never really liked ham or meat or how I imagined animals
coming back alive inside my body and taking their revenge.
My mind takes revenge. The thieves take their revenge,
and the television sets, jewelry, the money from our wallets,
and I dreamed last night that I was my man as a little boy
protecting his family from thieves. A big him inside
a little him inside of me protecting me, protecting us, protecting
the dog protecting us, and I wonder if the dog thinks of the world
as a great bathroom. Sometimes I have to pull my car into the shoulder
as the meat inside of me comes alive, galloping through my intestines,
roaring, kicking, and somewhere my grandfather
is doing a wheelie on the off-roads of heaven, hell,
or wherever he went all shiny and new like how my man
came to me, like how I imagined the Easter ham
as he zippered up his middle, lifted his sweet Easter head
and headed off the table and into the yard to roll in the sunshine
with the dogs. Right now I feel safe. The sun shall shine.
Spring has sprung and the buds have sent their stems through the dirt.

My man and I, we've made it through the winter, and my father
who lives 800 miles south made it through a few weeks ago.
But my mother, well, she lives a thousand miles north,
and she keeps telling me I ought to buy a motorcycle. I don't know
why.
I think sometimes she lives through me, vicariously. I think sometimes
she wants to ride off like grandpa. Galloping like a horse.
I think she wants to be shiny and new, wants to ride off past her bills,
her bad job, the yards in town on fire, right on
past her winter that's held her for years like a fist.

Jan LaPerle

Adventure, Adventure, Or Sit By The Door

My husband tells me nice things, so I iron his shirts
while it rains outside. I'm careful around his buttons.
Careful what I say. Careful around our baby
scooting across this floor. How dangerous I am
with this iron, how dangerous this mouth.
Our baby has his eyes; she is like a little spy,
an investigator of all things. She is simply smarter
than anyone I know. This morning she got stuck
under the piano bench and cried. I cry most days
over smaller things, but not today, even when
the hot buttons burn me. Because today I feel close
to my husband, even when he is not here; we are closer
than these fibers flattening beneath this iron—
this iron that a few minutes ago the baby was reaching for.
Our baby moves across these wooden floors like a broom.
When I lift her, she is covered in dirt and dog hair
and little strings that have fallen from our clothes.
How slowly we unravel; you'd hardly notice
if you were in here. The rain falls and falls.
We are terribly alone, this baby and I and when
I lift her she flips in my arms like a little fish.
I've told you before, our house is like a boat—
we float here. The rainwater fills our yard,
our basement: I'd like to think I am saving this baby,
keeping her from harm. Some people have said
our baby is sweet enough to eat, they stretch toward
her with their hands and teeth, but these people,
they are not here, they are trapped outside by the rain.
I iron and she sweeps. For a little while it is easy
to forget just how much floor spreads out in front of us,
how many shirts are wickedly wrinkled, how many people
are out there in cars and boots, muddying up this town.

Stitch

Sometimes, when I think of the Austrian daughter kept prisoner in the basement
by her father, I wonder if she learned to knit. Or, like me, if she preferred the stitch of
crochet—
a looser stitch, a lot like the pattern of a net. I wonder what *she* would catch. Catch,
catch, catch me if you can, I say when I let her free, when I let her run in the garden
with me. When she brushes against the flowering trees, blossoms fall,
and where they fall in the grasses the ground blooms—a pregnant ground,
a pregnant girl, and the babies move in her like candy & fruit.
I almost know she knits for those little melon heads with stitches tight as a noose.
Their cries are little songs: the only sound she hears from the outside world is that of the
locomotive!
I, too, hear the train from here as I slowly crochet a scarf, a net for my neck, strings
strung like a rope. I read yesterday about a war in China, how the men-soldiers strung
the naked women together by their necks like caught fish. I imagined their skin
in the sun glistening like fish. I hated to think they were so beautiful that way,
and I went to them on accident in the fog of a long gray dream dressed in my new sex,
where I moved through them like a locomotive.

Even in my dreams I feel guilty. But, still, they were only girls on paper: paper dolls
to slip over like a paper dress. And all at once they were pregnant.
When I pulled my hair from its pins it fell like water to the floor,
splashed in a pool like a skirt. I, too, was pregnant then, but when I walked from my
dream
I set down my pregnancy like a bag of groceries and woke: flat belly, flat, flat chest,
and my man behind me reaches with his big, big hands
for the big breasts of her ghost.

All these women are real to me. I catch them stitch-by-stitch. Lately I've begun to feel
their hair, corn silk between my fingers. Corn, corn, these women smell like corn,
and I eat them like a wild pig on the cob.

Wenze Wenze

I don't know what you did last weekend, but I spent my Saturday with a few prostitutes. I'm quite sure I'm not the only one who did so in this town, and I hope I'm not the only one who watched someone put a condom on.

I suspect, though, that my visit involved a bit more shouting and a bit less nudity than some others', though one can never be sure.

Who can tell me what this looks like? asks the community health worker.

Syphilis! shout the prostitutes.

I expect that these women are better at identifying the sexually-transmitted maladies shown on these horrific flash-card photos than most GPs.

Remember to get a good look at your partner's genitals in the light before you do it, the health worker continues, so you can check for sores.

The health worker holds up a box of condoms and the women cry *Wenze wenze!* "Everywhere, everywhere" in Lingala. *Wenze* alone refers to the small informal markets popping up all over town. "They're everywhere: get them, use them" is the message.

The box the health worker holds up is a box of three condoms, not unlike what's sold in the back corner of American pharmacies right next to the home pregnancy tests, an unsubtle hint. The three-condom box costs between fifty and a hundred Congolese francs or between ten and twenty US cents, depending on which neighborhood you're in and what time of night it is. A roll in the hay with one of the prostitutes sitting in front of me costs between eight hundred and 1000FC or around two dollars. A normal day for these women includes about eight clients. In a country where more than 75 percent of the country lives on less than a dollar a day, the money's not terrible.

These prostitutes are not like the ones I see in my neighborhood. They are not decked out in mini-skirts and heels and have not flashed me their wares because I drive a car with international license plates. They are between the ages of about twenty and forty-five and wear traditional *pagne* fabric tucked at the waist as they pull a toddler up onto their hips by the child's stray arm. They are not from Kinshasa. Some are slender and others are big African mamas with bellies. They are *villagois*, villagers.

The group laughs as two of the prostitutes roll-play a condom negotiation. In a culture where homosexuality is so taboo it's nonexistent, the "client" caresses the "prostitute's" breast unabashedly, offering an extra 500FC for the chance at skin on skin, flesh on flesh. *Come on. I'm not sick.* The prostitute agrees.

The health worker is disappointed. *Who can show me good condom negotiation skills?* A second pair of prostitutes approaches to give the roll-play a go. Once again, the "client" wins by topping up the offer. It's not until the third try that the condom wins out over the cash. *You might not be sick but you don't know who else I have been with. It's safer for us both.*

These lines ring familiar in my head and I wonder how many women in my own social circle have tried the same lines on their partners. Is there a line to trump every intelligent person out there who wants to negotiate condom use? Is there one line that makes us come undone and give up that which we know can protect us, can save our life? A dollar or a hundred dollars or an *I love you.*

We all slip up. We are human. But reality can be unforgiving. When a boyfriend and I agreed to ditch the condom, he looked me straight in the eye and said: *you realize you're trusting me with your life.* It doesn't get simpler than that.

A team from UN headquarters in New York interviewed me and a colleague of mine as a part of their study on sexual misconduct of UN Peace Keepers. The Peace Keepers are prohibited from having any type of sexual relationship with any Congolese as it's said to remove their objectivity as Peace

Keepers. You try telling 17,000 soldiers to keep it in their pants for a tour or two.

Needless to say, consorting is a given and the team from New York wanted to know where, how and what the acceptability is. My Congolese colleague who accompanied me to the meeting speculated that one in two or three female university students engage in some form of transactional sex. Boyfriends, some of whom are Peace Keepers, pay these women's way, buy them dinner and drinks and mobile phone credit. It's pocket money. These girls may be in a different class than the group sitting before the community health worker. They have prospects for the future. But the risks are not all that different

Wenze, wenze. There's a break in donor funds and in the coming months, condoms will be harder and harder to find in this city of 8 million. Wenze wenze. The HIV testing center these women are referred to has closed down and its transport vouchers are a memory. Wenze wenze.

I watch the condom demonstration as the prostitutes show off their expert application and removal skills with glee while their peers whoop in the background. They know what they're doing. They know the risks.

Wenze wenze.

Job Performance

reports of his
performance
cited delusions
of adequacy

he would video-
tape himself
changing bulbs
so bosses couldn't
claim god did it

he said,
the best thing
before sliced bread
obviously
was unsliced bread,
too easy

like a harp
he could be
unforgiving,
hard to get
in & out
of meetings

he believed
the difference
between a platonic kiss
&
an aristotelian one
had to do
with the feelings
of tragedy
inspired in the kissers

his mentor
was a screwdriver
that for him
turned nothing

his hopes
alternate endings

he said how long
a minute is
depends on what side
of the lightning
you're on

Gregor Samsa Plays The Flute

after Peter Marcek's "Spev zeme"

Gregor Samsa, the giant worm, was getting uglier and uglier as we drew nearer, and his stench was becoming unbearable. So we concentrated on the music, the wordless whimpering of a creature that had no eyes, no feet, and no hands. His sister held the flute close to his mouth. It looked as if he was about to swallow the musical instrument, but he held on. He huffed and puffed like no other great worm could. We did not see the pustules on his back as a result of him being bedridden for a long time. But the perforations on his body where black liquid trickled out were hard to miss. Gregor must have accidentally swallowed some twigs and sharp-edged indigestibles as some of them had pierced his belly. If he was not propped upright, we would not have known where his head was. If he did not insist on finishing whatever melody he was trying to conjure off that slime-slicked flute of his, we would never have known he was dying.

The Radio Gods Shuffle Their Feet

And how we longed to be trampled
in this carnage of screams and power chords,
of these mingled odors of sweat and misplaced
angst. We are whirring blades lost in each turn of hate.
We were young then, the parts of a tree which grew
so fast that they overburden their roots.
The stage lights dimmed. And when the amps
shrieked our rage, we would have cried to be
here, now and forever, would have died here
with them, with them, with our tiny radio gods
who played our songs, glorified our sicknesses.

Imprinting

Most days, I back off from the advancing frontline, that assembly of neighbors and friends trampling all the azaleas on my yard. They pretend to have their clothes on. They pretend to have names, hats, guidebooks, thermos flasks filled with coffee.

I smile, let them in
fully formed
or not.

Pottery

In another life I was pottery, matte terra cotta
and tall, up to my own ribcage. And filled.
Rock and soil to the brim, it created balance.

Imagine petals sprouting from the top
of your head. I stood in the sun on a sidewalk,
a town corner. Marigolds, white petunias,
bougainvillea flourished from my fontanelle,

caused people to pause, breathe deep, sometimes
to drag a palm along my bulbous midsection.
They ached for rough warmth, texture. They
savored the instant, the synapse. Memory never fails

here. There were faded striped awnings, and trimmed
trees whose leaves flickered chiaroscuro coins across
my orange belly at a certain time of day. And then

turquoise. I was an imperfect cube of bluegreen
in someone's hands, or many people's. A talisman.

An Ode to My Mother and the Four Dead Bunnies

May 2009: Beauty and the Sun.

I came home this morning to find my mother crying.

The forty-five minute drive from my boyfriend's house to home felt shorter than usual. The seven am sun was beautiful. Even the dirty street corners glistened. I don't remember many days that looked, or felt, the way this morning did. There was no one to miss. People or ghosts. Not even time that has long since passed. In fact, I was happy. I was happy until I came home to find my mother curled up on the black leather couch, head cupped into her oversized hands with tears and saliva running through the cracks of her fingertips. Suddenly the day became similar to many other days and nights and weeks. Some days there is a comfort in the familiar, but not today. Not when I had such a great morning in comparison. The couch sits in the middle of the sunlight pouring in through the large bay window. She had the fans turned off and I felt the heat the second I walked into the room. The sun hitting the sweat on her body made her skin sparkle like an angel and for a moment it occurred to me that she had never looked so beautiful.

Late 1980's-Early 1990's: Disco Balls and Mutants

My sister, Lisa, was born July 1983 during one of the worst thunderstorms Northeast Ohio had even seen. From what I understand, the entire city of Medina lost power. My sister was like a bolt of lightning. Our mother was twenty years old. Sometimes I fantasize that the storm was some sort of message or warning from God for the changes coming in my mother's life. God might do that, right? Or maybe it was just a coincidence that she gave birth to her new life during the storm and God had nothing to do with it. Realistically,

God probably wouldn't waste his time on us. Two and a half years later I was born. At twenty-three years old my mother had two young girls, strangers, she was forced to learn to love and raise.

At twenty-five years old my mother was still beautiful and decided that her life was too restricting. She still had so much in her: so much life left to live (although today I feel that she just watched too many movies and felt she was part of the cliché). She needed freedom. She couldn't stay at home and take care of us night after night while my dad worked the third shift as a mechanic. She wanted to go to the night clubs and dance under the disco balls and drink cheap beer with strangers who wanted things from her she shouldn't have given, while she left my sister and I on an old ratty couch in front of the bay window with a baby sitter named Danielle.

At twenty-seven years old my mother's face was ripped off her skull. She was on her way home late at night and fell asleep at the wheel, veering off to the left of State Route 83 into a cement barrier.

At thirty years old my mutated mother loved us, maybe for the first time. But who am I to say? I was too young to really remember much. I do remember that she let us rent all the scary movies we wanted. She stayed up late at night with us eating ice cream and blue and red freezer pops. In front of that bay window on the new soft black couch, the three of us formed one big lump under the blue fleece blanket that made our legs itch. We were happy.

December 1994: Swollen Eyelids and Make Believe Women.

She always cried in the winter. Seasonal depression, she called it. She said it was the lack of sunlight that brought her down. She began to lock herself in the bedroom on the weekends. She avoided the bay window and the soft black couch most of the time, unless we were having the occasional family meeting.

The family meetings, consisting of only me, Lisa, and her sitting on the couch facing the bay window looking at the empty street and large elm tree off to the right:

"I am going to ask you girls something and I need you to answer me honestly, do you understand?" Her face was swollen as she had spent the morning crying in her bedroom.

"Okay. We won't lie," we said in unison. We thought we were on trial, sitting there with our knees bent and our hands clasped tightly between our thighs. Had she found out about the mud fight we had or maybe it was that we overflowed the bath tub two days before?

"Have you ever seen a woman out in your father's barn?" Her eyes were set on our foreheads, as she was too ashamed to make eye contact.

"A woman?" Lisa's voice broke. "What do you mean a woman?" Her arms were skinny like mine and I watched her muscles flex as she grasped her knees.

"I mean a woman. Any woman." Mom's eyes began to moisten all over again as she placed her large hands together with her thumbs on her chin.

"You mean you think Daddy is cheating on you?" My sister grabbed my hand and held it tight while I wondered how many minutes of how many days of how many years it took for the elm outside to grow so big.

Summer 1995: Dead Ends.

I think of this summer as the summer of the yellow grass. It was so hot and there was so little rain. Everything seemed dehydrated and deflated. My mother made up a game for me and Lisa to play. It was called Sneakies. We were to dedicate all of our spare time to it. The object of the game was to not be seen by Dad or any of his workers in the barn. We were to sneak around and find the woman hiding somewhere in the barn. She was there, Mom was certain of it. Whoever found the lady first, would win the nickname of Carman San Diego.

June 2000: Red Wine Summer.

I was in love with a red headed boy and completely unaware of my mother's past. The scars left on her face were something left behind from a battle of morals where she was in the right and the bad guy cried himself to sleep every night. The summer was hot and the pressure was building with the red head. I was bound to cave. Maybe it was even destined that for the next nine years I would think of him and our first time whenever UB40's "Red Red Wine" played on the radio in a car, or in the line at a fast food restaurant, or at my grand parents' anniversary party. Time after time, feeling the beads of sweat form where my hair line met my forehead.

When I wasn't in the basement with the red head that summer, I was with my mother. We spent our Saturdays together driving an hour and a half to Brook Park to visit Grandma Irene. On our way home we would stop at the movie theatre and watch two movies in a row. I remember the car rides most. If it was nice outside we would roll the windows down and I would carefully place my head out the window, feeling the wind against my face. If it was cold or rainy we would sing 80's music together and the windows would fog but we would just keep singing like something you would see in an indie movie.

Mom was in her late thirties then. She was heavy, as she called herself an "emotional eater." Her cheek bones were round and melted in with her chin, but her hair was long and beautiful and managed to compliment her face, giving her a beauty she didn't see. Couldn't see. I didn't know there was anything wrong then. How could I not have known?

We were sitting in front of the bay window when I told her about "Red Red Wine." She cried and her tears ran down the leftover scars on her face. I cried. And we never mentioned it again.

May 14, 2005: The Game.

The night of the Green Day concert. I woke up that morning with pink eye, and I like to think that maybe it was God's way of warning me not to go out that night. Ha, God. Like my mother and the lady in the barn, I have this indistinct notion of God; a God who loves without discrimination and warns someone before they are walking off the plank and into the moat of crocodiles with razor sharp teeth. Or driving down the highway in the pouring rain, wanting nothing more than to throw the car into the cement barrier and kill everyone it.

Mom was fine during the concert. I remember the way her hair fell behind her ears while she was danced and sang to the *American Idiot* album, maybe trying to relive her nightclub days. My sister and I were even having a good time. It was a large arena and I remember looking around and seeing nothing but a pool of colors and thinking about how hard it was to fathom that it was actually made up of individual people. I wondered if any of the people had a bay window or a life like mine or a history like my mother.

After the show, we were looking for the car, walking aimlessly around Cleveland when my mother unexpectedly broke the silence.

"I need you to drop me off at your Uncle's on the way home. I need to talk to him." Her voice was now hoarse, that familiar hoarse that meant she was going to crack at any time.

"Mom, it is almost two in the morning. I'm not going to drop you off there. He's sleeping. Why don't you just call him in the morning?"

I was already stressed about not being able to find the car, the last thing I wanted was to try to explain the ridiculousness of the request to her.

"No, you are going to drop me off. I need to talk to him *tonight*—" At this she started to cry.

"Mom what's the matter? Why can't you just talk to him tomorrow?" Lisa was gentle. Soothing, even. Unlike me, she wasn't annoyed. She was worried.

"Just stop! Don't talk down to me! You girls don't understand! I need to talk to him about the *government!*" She was hysterical, putting her hands in the air and stomping her feet.

I stopped dead in my tracks and placed my hands over my face. I was at a loss. My inner gut wanted me to scream at her. Scream to her she was a sloppy drunk and was making finding the car a hell of a lot more difficult than it needed to be. I wanted to tell her that I couldn't take her seriously when she was drunk and irrational. I almost wanted to laugh in her face, and I would've if I thought it would have made a difference.

"Mom. Listen to me," I rarely sound as mean as I did at that moment. "We are *not* going to take you to see him. You are drunk and need to settle down. Once we find the car you can go to sleep and I'll drive us home. Then you can get in bed and sleep this off—" The yellow traffic lights gave a false sense of hope. We were lost in a dark unfamiliar city.

"No, you listen to me. I am *not* getting in bed with your father. Not tonight, not ever again. Thinking about his hands on my body make me want to slice his throat with a rusty machete. I need to see my brother. He understands. He *listens* to me." At this she let her two hundred and fifty pound body fall to the sidewalk. She wrapped her arms around her head and began to cry. "I have to fucking pee. I need to find a fucking bathroom." She looked pathetic. Drunk, sweaty, and pathetic. I imagined Dad lying on the road with his throat slit, the sliced skin looking thick like skin should as the blood poured over his neck, his shoulders, and created a large red pool on the asphalt.

We finally found the car.

The highway was dark. Almost black, I imagine it must have been a new moon. Or maybe the lights of the teal blue Lincoln were playing God, telling me I should drive the car into the cement barrier. Lisa sat in the backseat, through the rear view mirror I saw the beads of sweat running down her hairline. Our two hundred and fifty pound mother was stretched out with her head on Lisa's lap, crying.

Diving the Lincoln in the rain, watching the rain drops slam onto the windshield, the last thing I wanted to do was cry or try to make her feel better. I wanted to drive the car into a barrier and kill all of us. I wanted to have my legs severed when I flew through the windshield, and I wanted to lie on the wet pavement in the rain, next to my mom, who would have to see what she had done to me as she breathed her last breath of cold, wet air and choked on her own vomit.

"I want to know who the *fuck* is paying you two to drive me crazy," Mom redefined crying uncontrollably, "do you think it's funny? And why are my parents trying to poison me? They invite me over every Friday night for dinner so they can put rat poison in my food. I know it but I keep eating it anyway because I don't care if I die! I want to die! I hate both of you, I wish I had never had you! And I hate my parents. I wish they never had me! I hate everyone..."

I heard Lisa shushing her while she ran her fingers through Mom's greasy hair and cried with her. She cried *with* her. I stared at the highway trying not to think about the fact that I hated my mother, just as she hated her mother. I would never be able to be in the backseat crying. I thought back to the years that led up to this point and realized I had not seen any warning signs. Nothing I took seriously. I didn't take her seriously. I couldn't. One week she was laughing and taking me out to early breakfasts on Saturdays and the next she was locked away in her room sitting on that old green recliner in the dark staring into space. How had I not seen these as signs? I should've known this was coming.

The rain was bombing the windshield and the glare of the headlights on the street made it difficult to see.

"I fucking pissed myself. How does that make you girls feel?"

Mom was sitting up now, trying to open the door of the car and jump out. I locked the door instinctively, knowing she was too drunk to figure out how to open it. I imagined her large body falling out the door and rolling across the highway. "I care about people. I really do. I try to care. I think about all of the less fortunate people and I cry at night. I care. Stop thinking I don't, because I do."

Her anger turned into a pathetic attempt of apathy as I heard her sucking snot back into her nose through uncontrollable sobs. "I hate your fucking father. I know he is fucking women in the barn and I fucking hate him for it. And I see people sometimes, looking in the kitchen window. I need privacy, I need out of that Goddamn house. You are all trying to kill me, and I know it. Just stop the fucking car!"

I wanted to hit the eject button and watch a better movie. Fuck rewinding or fast forwarding. I needed a new movie completely. A movie that didn't have me driving a car with a Mom who apparently needed a lot of help—more help than I was going to be able to give her; a movie where I wasn't the daughter who didn't take the time to see the signs of her mother's schizophrenia.

When we finally got home that night, I let her and my sister out of the car, both thinking I would be right behind them. Instead I drove to a twenty-four-hour country kitchen with dirty carpets and sad servers who wanted to be anywhere but working at an empty restaurant at one in the morning. I sat at a booth while I cried and held onto my stomach, trying to squeeze out the rot I felt eating away my insides. Hours went by. Hours and hours and hours. The sun came up, and I still sat there drinking one cup of coffee after another. I imagined abandoning everyone and everything I knew and living happily with a clean slate. I could forget them.

I was so scared to go home.

The next morning I stood next to Dad in the kitchen. Dad the mechanic with the strong hands and permanent smile. Dad the jokester. The man who never ever had a woman hiding in the barn, or a woman other than my mom at all. I wanted to hug him while he looked vacantly at the white tiled countertop.

I didn't hug him. I just stared at the tile and watched as his tears began to fall like atomic bombs.

Lisa later told me that when her and Mom got into the house that night, Mom ran up the carpeted stairs and through the narrow hallway and slammed her fists against her and Dad's bedroom door as hard as she could, screaming that she was going to slit his throat in his sleep, her large body engrossing the door and sliding to the floor. Then she cried. And cried. And cried some more.

I moved out the following August. I would've moved sooner had I found someone to split rent with. I transferred colleges and got an apartment eighty miles away from her. I talked to her as little as possible and when I did I was at a distance. She was no longer my mother. She was a stranger trying to play the part.

Spring Semester 2006: Stuck on crazy.

I was so stuck on her and the concept of being truly sick. What is sick? Has our society really advanced to such a degree that we are able to diagnose one another as normal and sick? Abnormal. Crazy. If you are either, you should be medicated. She refused. And who defines crazy? How do you tell someone they aren't *right*. How do you tell someone that their reasoning isn't rational? But what is rational? Am I worthy to judge? How do I really feel about medication, about her becoming a product of a pill she swallows? Was her insistence on moving to Florida to live in a trailer alone with her dog crazy? Was it crazy to want to die in a trailer alone with your dog in Florida?

I decided to write a list of the things I loved about her; or at least at one time in the past had loved.

1. Her laugh. It was a ridiculous laugh and probably the deepest laugh I have ever heard.
2. Her smile. Even through the scar left behind from her accident, she had a smile I associated with only her.
3. Scary movie nights. Freddy. Jason. Dolls. Hellraiser. Prom Night. The nightmares Lisa and I would have and tell Mom about the next morning.
4. The couch cushion castles and our drives to Grandma's.
5. Our bay window.

My eyes began to burn like one of the old campfires and tears began to roll down my cheeks. I missed her. Maybe I had left the game too soon.

I moved back home for the last two years of college. I rebuilt my relationship with my mom, as much as a relationship can be rebuilt. There have been quite a few episodes since, but not as bad as the first. Or maybe I have just become immune.

One white December night, sitting at the white tiled counter in our kitchen, I told her she was sick. She looked out the window, her body completely still. I told her we loved her and were afraid for her. There was no reason she should be living so miserably when medication would help her. She was silent. So silent. For so long.

Minutes and minutes passed before I told her there was no one looking in our windows and that the government didn't have hidden cameras in our house. She didn't look at me, but shook her head. The only sound in the entire house was that of her tears falling onto the tile.

May 2009: The Crying Pill and the Bunnies.

I came home this morning and I found her crying on the couch.

"Mom, what's the matter?" I walked over to the floor fan and plugged it into the outlet behind the television.

"Oh Shells, they died. I tried so…hard."

She had found four baby bunnies the day before and had been bottle feeding them every two hours.

"You know, Mom, it's really hard to nurse wild animals, especially when they're babies. You remember all the times we tried doing it as kids? They never made it."

"I thought this time was going to be different. I thought I could do it."

"It's the point that you tried, Mom." I leaned over, gave her a tissue, and hugged her.

A little over an hour later, I walked out onto the back porch to go to my car. Out of the corner of my eye I saw a couch pillow on the picnic table. I walked over and saw the four dead bunnies, placed on the pillow in a cross with their heads facing one another, bathing in the sun.

Peter Branson

The Boat House

London Rowing Club, Putney

This is the season for it, not when fields
are iced iron-rut or frayed brown corduroy
or loud with corn; rather when bells are pitched
to tune with living things, the rising sap,
white blossom, throstle, lark, hormonal rooks.
These days the stallion's bolted, door distressed -
I'm speaking generally of course — and yet
it's not died out nor been replaced. Young folk
don't change that much, still feel the need to pledge
their troth in front of family and friends,
the world to judge. So what of this bright pair
who've pulled us here today, twin oars - one boat?
They've chosen well I think, each other, this,
the food and drink, the company, the view.

Contributors

Annie Strong (cover) is the singer of the Chicago-based punk band This Is My Fist. She is currently applying to veterinary schools.

Jude Bradley has been a journalist for 35 years and currently teaches creative writing and screenwriting in Palmdale, California. *Magic's In the Bag* (Llewellyn Worldwide 2010) co-authored by Chere Dastugue Coen, is her most recent book. For six years, she worked on the editorial desk at *Variety*. She currently freelances as a writer, editor, designer, producer and spiritual consultant. She hold degrees in Journalism, Visual Arts and Administration of Justice.

Judy Jordan's first book of poetry, *Carolina Ghost Woods*, won the National Book Critics Circle Award, the Academy of American Poets Walt Whitman Award, the Thomas Wolfe Literary Award, the Oscar Arnold Young Book Prize of the Poetry Council of North Carolina, and the Utah Book of the Year Award for Poetry.

Her second volume, a book-length poem, *60 Cent Coffee and a Quarter to Dance* was released in 2005 by Louisiana State University Press. Her third manuscript *Hunger,* which centers around two years of semi-homelessness during which she lived in a half-collapsed greenhouse is with Louisiana State University press. A vegan, Jordan currently lives off-grid, surrounded by the Shawnee National Forest in a Thoreau-size cordwood cabin she built herself and is completing an eco-friendly, passive solar heated, hybrid earthbag and cob house. She is nearing completion of a fourth book of poetry and is working on a memoir and a work of non-fiction concerning global climate change. She is a professor of poetry at Southern Illinois University Carbondale.

Ricky Ginsburg is one of those writers who sees a flock of birds heading south for the winter and wonders what they talk about on their journey. His portfolio consists of over 200 short stories, half of which have found their way into various magazines, both paper and electronic, and four novels, as yet unpublished. While much of his writing has elements of magical realism and humor, he also has a serious side, but keeps it in a small Plexiglas box under his desk.

Amy Holwerda the nonfiction editor of *Shady Side Review*, a literary journal published out of Pittsburgh where she recently earned her MFA. Selections of my work have appeared in *The Sycamore Review, The Collagist, Quick Fiction, Flash International,* and my chapbook, *The Grayest Ghost,* among others.

KB Ballentine A graduate of Lesley University's MFA program, KB has attended writing academies in both America and Britain. Published in *Alehouse, Bent Pin, Front Range, Long Story Short,* and others, she shares her work in various poetry groups. A finalist for the 2007 Ruth Stone Prize in Poetry and the 2006 Joy Harjo Poetry Award, she was awarded monies from the Dorothy Sargent Rosenberg Memorial Fund in 2006 and 2007. In February 2008, Celtic Cat Publishing debuted KB's first collection of poetry *Gathering Stones* and in 2009 released her second collection *Fragments of Light.*

Rich Murphy's credits include the 2008 Gival Press Poetry Award for *Voyeur,* a first book, *The Apple in the Monkey Tree;* chapbooks, *Great Grandfather, Family Secret, Hunting and Pecking, Rescue Lines,* and *Phoems for Mobile Vices;* poems in *Rolling Stone, Poetry, Grand Street, Trespass, New Letters, Pank, Segue, EOAGH, Big Bridge, Pemmican, foam:e,* and *Confrontation;* and essays in *The International Journal of the Humanities, Reconfigurations: A Journal for Poetics Poetry / Literature and Culture, Journal of Ecocriticism, Fringe, Folly Magazine,* among others. Rich lives in Marblehead, MA.

Tracy Haught earned a BA in English literature and creative writing from Cameron University. Her work has appeared in *The Oklahoma Review, Poetry For The Masses, Polyphony, Sugar Mule, Magnapoets, The Whistling Fire,* and was anthologized in *"Aint Nobody That Can Sing Like Me."* She won the Matt Haag fiction contest in 2007 for her short story "Beyond Bonnie's House," and again in 2009 for her story "Where We Come From." Tracy has written two novels, both works of literary fiction. She resides in Pennsylvania's Lehigh Valley with her husband, Deron, her two children, Jackson and Emma, and her two dogs, Badge and Story.

Adam Tavel won the 2010 Robert Frost Award, and his recent poems appear or are forthcoming in *Indiana Review, Phoebe, Redivider, The Los Angeles Review, Cave Wall,* and *The Minnesota Review,* among others. He lives and teaches on Maryland's Eastern Shore.

Michael Ryan lives in the suburban Washington D.C. area where he has been a middle school counselor for eleven years. He is currently working on a short story collection, as well as querying agents for his novel. This is his first publication. He would like to thank his family and writing group, especially Kevin, for all their support and encouragement.

Sequoia Nagamatsu's stories have appeared in ZYZZYVA, *Gargoyle, The Bellevue Literary Review,* The *New Delta Review, climate,* and *One World: A Global Anthology of Short Stories* (New Internationalist, Oxford). He is pursuing an MFA in creative writing at Southern Illinois University in Carbondale.

Sybil Baker is the author of *Talismans* and *The Life Plan.* Her short stories and essays have appeared in numerous journals and anthologies including *Prairie Schooner, upstreet,* and *The Writer's Chronicle.* She received her MFA from the Vermont College of Fine Arts. After living in South Korea for twelve years, she now lives in Chattanooga, Tennessee, where she is an Assistant Professor of English.

Rick Marlatt holds two degrees from the University of Nebraska, as well as a MFA from the University of California, Riverside, where he served as poetry editor of *The Coachella Review.* Marlatt's first book, *How We Fall Apart,* was the winner of the 2010 Seven Circle Press poetry chapbook award. His most recent work appears in *New York Quarterly, Rattle,* and *Anti.* Marlatt writes poetry reviews for *Coldfront Magazine,* and he teaches English in Nebraska, where he lives with his wife and two sons.

Margaret Elysia Garcia won 2nd place in the 34th Annual National Chicano/Latino Literary Award given by the University of California for her short story collection 605 Freeway Stories; a story of hers was a

Glimmer Train finalist earlier this year. "Gordita's Ride" is part of the collection. Her work can be seen in *Best Fiction, Underground Voices, Antique Children, The Sun,* and other small literary places. She lives in exile from her past lives in a remote corner of the Sierra Mountains. You can follow her adventures on her blog, Tales of a Sierra Madre www.writerchick-mama.blogspot.com

James Valvis the author of *How to Say Goodbye* (Aortic Books, 2011). His writing can be found in *Arts & Letters, Atlanta Review, Confrontation, Elimae, GHLL, LA Review, Rattle, River Styx, and is forthcoming in Anderbo, Crab Creek Review, Daily Science Fiction, Hanging Loose, Midwest Quarterly, New York Quarterly, South Carolina Review,* and others. His poetry has been featured at *Verse Daily* and the Best American Poetry blog. His fiction has twice been a storySouth Million Writers Notable Story. He lives near Seattle with his wife and daughter.

Kate Moening is from Portland, Oregon and is thrilled to be included in *Prime Mincer's* summer issue. She graduated from Grinnell College and currently lives in Alaska.

David Morris Parson has published stories in *Queen City Review, Wilderness House Literary Review,* and *The Meadowland Review,* among others. When he is not working on my novel and short stories, he writes TV commercials for a national advertising agency.

MJ Nicholls is a firm believer in the brief bio. He lives in Edinburgh and writes fiction and its opposite.

Abigail Hines graduated from Ball State University with a B.A. in telecommunications. She likes to read anything by Lorrie Moore, drink Dr. Pepper, and dance around like she's being electrocuted. When she grows up, she wants to be a film director, a non-fiction writer, and a nurse. Also, she has three cats. You can read her most recent work in the current issue of *Anatomy, (nano)Specter* and *Chamber Four.*

David Kawrykow was born in Germany and recently completed a master's degree in software engineering at McGill University. He currently works at an investment bank.

Valery Petrovskiy is a journalist and short story writer from Russia. He studied English at Chuvash State University, Cheboksary and journalism at VKSch Higher School, Moscow. He has been writing prose since 2005. Some of his work has been published in *The Scrambler, Rusty Typer, BRICKrethoric, NAP Magazine, Literary Burlesque, The Other Room, Curbside Quotidian, DANSE MACABRE, WidowMoon Press* He lives in a remote village in Chuvash Republic, Russia.

Rob Schultz taught literature and composition at Western Michigan University and Virginia Commonwealth University before drifting into radio and voice work. He published his first novel, *Styll in Love*, over a decade ago (Van Neste Books, 1998). He is currently seeking a publisher for another novel, "On-Air," and book of collected stories, "In Hart." Other work has appeared in a number of literary journals, including *Slant, The MacGuffin, Rattapallax, Sou'wester* and *West Branch*.

Jan LaPerle is originally from a small town in northern New Hampshire, but currently lives in the mountains of East Tennessee with her husband and daughter. Her work is published or forthcoming in *Dislocate, Rattle, Boxcar Poetry Review, PANK, Tusculum Poetry Review, Tar River Poetry Review, Subtropics, Birmingham Poetry Review*, and elsewhere.

Kate Wolf is a public health worker who's been living in Africa for the better part of the last ten years. She writes about it when she can, when she's inspired and when she has something to write that won't result in her getting deported.

Mathhew Guenette, born in Syracuse, NY, grew up in Newport, NH. He has worked as a dishwasher, short-order cook, busboy, landscaper, day-laborer, in an art gallery, and for a standardized testing company grading essays written by grade-schoolers from Kentucky. He was raised by a single mother, Karen Pasanen Guenette Arnoldy Schneider, for which he has a myriad of memories, many sweet, some conflicting. He lost his virginity at age 16. Harvard, the Iowa Writer's Workshop, and Johns Hopkins are a few of the prestigious and excellent institutions he was neither smart enough to attend as a student nor accomplished enough now, as a writer, to teach for. After being kicked out of Syracuse University for academic craptitude, he moved to Dubuque, Iowa, worked two months in a plastic factory under a racist manager, dropped acid, and lost $2000--an inheritance from a deceased uncle--in quick fashion at riverboat casinos. He considers himself a collagist, using avante-garde techniques to produce accessible, narrative poems. As an extra in the film *Public Enemies* he can be seen for .37 seconds standing behind J. Edgar Hoover, played by Billy Crudup. His dream home would be on the shores of Lake Superior, which reminds him of the ocean back east. He wore a tutu once as a prank, and another time assless chaps. He has screws in his left hip and knee, the result of surgeries the result of a once athletic lifestyle. When pressed, he lacks the courage to identify himself as an atheist, hedging instead with the safer agnostic. He is married, to a woman much smarter and far more patient, with two beautiful, maddening children. When his mother died he stood at her bedside, his hands resting on her arm, and often makes the not-exactly right comparison of the sound of her last breaths to that of a stringed instrument being tuned in a far-away room. He is the author of two books: *American Busboy* (U. of Akron Press, 2011) and *Sudden Anthem* (Dream Horse Press, 2008). He lives, works, loses sleep in Madison, WI., is happy to be here, and is grateful to the editors at *Prime Mincer.*

Kristine Ong Muslim has more than five hundred publications including *Boston Review, Contrary Magazine, Harpur Palate, Narrative Magazine, Potomac Review, Sou'wester, Southword,* and *The Pedestal Magazine.* She has been nominated five times for the Pushcart Prize and twice for *Best of the Web 2011.*

Sandy Fontana received her MFA from Southern Illinois University Carbondale. At SIUC, she won The Academy of American Poets Prize in 2002, 2003, and 2004. Her poetry is published in nationally recognized literary magazines. At Shawnee Community College, Sandy teaches developmental writing, English composition, introductory literature and poetry classes, and creative writing.

Michelle Wotowiec has recently completed her English MA at Cleveland State University. Some of her other work can be found in Scribes Valley Publishing's anthologies *Welcome to Elsewhere* and *Visiting Elsewhere* (www.scribesvalley.com). Her achievements include three publications to date.

Michelle believes in writing without limits and without censorship: write from your gut and love what you write. She would like to thank her mother and the rest of her family for the love and support they have given her throughout her writing career.

Thank you.

www.ingramcontent.com/pod-product-compliance
Lightning Source LLC
Chambersburg PA
CBHW051514170626
46811CB00002B/823